THE YEAR
OF THE
LORD

The Church Year:

Its Customs, Growth, & Ceremonies

THEODORE J. KLEINHANS

Concordia Publishing House

Saint Louis

BOOKS by the same author

Martin Luther: Saint and Sinner

Alone with God

Printer's Devil from Wittenberg

The Music Master: J. S. Bach

Talking with God

Time of Testing

Letters to John

Scoutways to God

Member, Authors Guild

Concordia Publishing House, St. Louis, Missouri
Concordia Publishing House Ltd., London, E. C. 1
© 1967 by Concordia Publishing House

Library of Congress Catalog Card No. 67-14768

MANUFACTURED IN THE UNITED STATES OF AMERICA

For

Chris

and

Kit

Preface

This book concerns itself chiefly with the church year — the year of the Lord. It also concerns itself with other elements of faith that are connected with the church year — worship in general, liturgy, the propers, vestments, hymnody, architecture, folklore, and customs.

It is intended for the general reader, and for that reason I have ruled out any thought of footnotes. I have no doubt that it will contain errors — errors both of interpretation and of fact. Even for these I follow in noble footsteps.

The Venerable Bede wrongly thought that Easter was named after a Germanic goddess of Spring, Eostre, though no one has ever found another reference to such a goddess. But who knows — some runic inscription older than the *Wessobrunner Gebet* may still appear and prove Bede right. And St. Bonaventure, whose writings, in the process of canonization, were approved as "without error," gives Francis of Assisi credit for starting the Christmas crèche, though Rome had already known similar crèches for centuries.

I first worked out this manuscript on an island in the Azores, far from anything that resembled a theological library, with all due respect for the Portuguese tomes of the archbishop of Angra. Fortunately I could beg or borrow copies of authorities like Strodach, Dix, Horn, Parsch, Underhill, Cabrol, Shepherd, Weiser, Jungmann, Duchesne, and Schmemann, and to them I am grateful not only for much of what appears in this book but also for a whole new insight into the life of the church. May what I have written in turn help you to understand your own faith and worship.

Biloxi, Mississippi
Embertide 1966

Introduction

When the patriarch Noah climbed down from the ark, he first built an altar and offered sacrifice. What Noah was really doing, in liturgical language, was *celebrating* — celebrating the love of God that had spared him from the watery depths, remembering the covenant God had made with him, recalling those long days on the ark when he and his were the only remaining symbols of the Creator's hand.

The glory of the Hebrew faith was a sense of awe for the mighty Jehovah, an awe that kept man from writing out God's name or even pronouncing it. It was a love and respect for the God of the fathers, of Abraham, Isaac, and Jacob; the God who had called His people out of Egypt; the God who had summoned Moses to Sinai; the God who had routed the armies of Sennacherib.

This relationship permeated the whole life of the chosen people, every minute and week and season, or as God expressed it to Noah, "While the earth remains," through "seedtime and harvest, cold and heat, summer and winter, day and night."

The worship of the Jews was above all else one of recalling, remembering, and celebrating. It was an acting out of what had happened in the past. It was a ceremonious telling of father to son, lest the glories of a bounteous Lord ever ceased to be sung, or His name ceased to be praised.

The greatest of the Jewish religious rites was the Passover, an occasion when the Scriptures were not merely read out and explained, as they were each day by rote in the home or each week from the scrolls in the synagog, but actually acted out.

The firstborn son in a special way felt that he had been spared by God's avenging angel. His brothers and sisters shared in some of the sorrow of Egypt as they ate of the bitter herbs. The entire family sensed that it was *they,* and not just their fathers, who had been delivered out of the house of bondage. In the figure of the Paschal Lamb they all awaited Him whom they called the Messiah—the Anointed.

This sense of remembering and of acting out one's faith is basic to the whole concept of Christian worship and of the Christian year. This is exactly what Peter and Paul and James were doing when they gathered their little flocks together after Pentecost.

Remembering Christ in this special way is central to worship even now. We do it when we read of His mighty acts, when we sing His praises, when we bring Him our petitions, when we offer the fruits of our hands, and in the most meaningful way of all, when we share in His real presence in the body and blood of the Holy Supper.

Because it is so distinctly related to the present, to the here and now, this remembering is not merely historical. It is a living part of the present, not just a memento of the past. It is the actualization of God's mighty acts. It is not the same as remembering the 700th anniversary of Dante or the 400th of Shakespeare.

Gathered in Christ's name, we become one with all who have ever worshiped, we even become one with God Himself, and His saving acts become a present reality. This is why in our worship we can address Him as the One acting here and now: "The Lord *Is* My Shepherd," "Joy to the World, the Lord *Is* Come," "Christ the Lord *Is* Risen *Today.*"

God, who is Himself beyond time, chose the fullness of time to send His Son into our midst. Because mankind lives in a world of time, it is only natural that in worship we should also follow the patterns of time.

This the church has always done, whether in the time of the Old Covenant or the New. In worship we need pattern and repetition, even as we need it in our eating and sleeping. We need the tangible and the material—whatever will help us, whether it be a roof to keep the snow off our heads, a candle, a cross, or an organ.

Religious symbols and actions have always been at home in the house of God, and though they are not magical or sacred in themselves, they lead us closer to the great mystery of a God who revealed Himself as flesh of our flesh and blood of our blood.

Unlike the legendary statue of Diana, which gave Paul such a difficult time at Ephesus, forms and patterns of worship did not fall from heaven. They are man-made. They are therefore subject to change and even to ambiguity and error. And yet they are also sacred, for they help us exercise ourselves in thanksgiving to God, and in this way liturgy and the observance of the church year keep us near Him. The Greek Church has a fine phrase for worship in "the divine liturgy"—

translatable as the "divine public good," the "divine public work," the "divine public worship."

The philosophy of the Lutheran reformers, as summarized in the Formula of Concord, states well the whole concept of public worship. Times and seasons of the year, hours and days, vestments, orders of worship are not in themselves sacred, except insofar as they help draw us near to the One who Himself dwelled in the holy of holies. Yet down through the centuries the experience and judgment of a whole cloud of witnesses have taught us how we can worship Him who is above all time and beyond all space. When we draw on the treasures of the past, we do what Paul suggested to the faithful at Thessalonike, "Hold fast that which is good."

Contents

I

The Growth of the Church Year

REGULARITY OF WORSHIP

Already in the Garden of Eden man worshiped his Maker in an orderly and patterned way—as creature and Creator communed together in the cool of the evening and as they rested together on the seventh day. Right from the beginning Adam and Eve worshiped the Lord daily in all they thought and did, and in a special way weekly.

Already in the account of Cain and Abel there is an indication of a yearly cycle of worship, the church year. When the sons of Adam offered God the firstfruits of their flocks and fields, they showed that worship was already related to seedtime and harvest, the natural flow of the seasons.

Their pattern of worship was a natural one, based on what they did, whether by day, week, month, or year. In tent, tabernacle, or temple, God's chosen people sang His praises, confessed their faults, and offered their sacrifices, all as they awaited the coming of the Messiah.

When God's own Son became flesh of our flesh and when the Old Covenant between God and man was forever replaced by the New, the faithful naturally centered their worship on the life of Christ. Yet worship never really lost the basic elements it had known among the Jews—the sense of awe at the presence of God, the ecstatic outbursts of praise, the overpowering mood of guilt, the closeness to God in one's daily work, the vision of hope that only God can offer.

All this seems centuries removed from worship as we know it now. And yet there is much in common between a pious Hebrew of the time of Christ and a faithful Christian of the 20th century. Every Passover a good Jew could transport himself into the world of a slave who was delivered from Egypt, with all the reverence and trust of one who had lived through such a harrowing experience. Every Easter a Christian can step into the trembling sandals of St. John in the morning dew outside the open tomb.

If faith is real, we should be aware of God as we mow the lawn, wash the dishes, shovel snow, or peel potatoes. The church year, as it recites the experience of others who knew God in their lives, is intended to help us experience Him in our own.

At Advent we join Isaiah and David as they hymn the coming Messiah. At Christmas we hasten with the shepherds to behold the Child in the manger. At Epiphany we add our gifts to those of the Wise Men. At Palm Sunday we wave fronds and sing hosannas. At Easter we rise early with the Marys to witness the miracle of the tomb. At Ascension we stare nostalgically at the place where our Lord has gone.

Once Christ had ascended to His Father and sent His Holy Spirit, there were two events the disciples could not forget — the Resurrection and the Passover. Once they came to realize what it meant that their Lord was no longer dead but alive, they began to understand the love and concern He had tried to express to them when He had promised He would never leave them.

In the mind of the young church the Resurrection and the Passover meal were not two events but one, culminating of course on Easter. Right from the start the church did as the Lord had commanded her — it gave thanks for His continuing presence and awaited His return as triumphant Judge, at the same time acting out what He had done there in the Upper Room on that first Maundy Thursday.

SUNDAY

To the Hebrew the seventh day of the week was the Sabbath, a day when he rested from his labors and worshiped his God. But to the early disciples the rest was not so important as the worship, as Jesus had clearly pointed out when He used the Sabbath, after a proper explanation, to heal the crippled and to harvest wheat.

What made Sunday the cornerstone of Christian worship, of the church year, and even of faith itself was what happened on Easter. As Paul put it, if Christ had not been raised, we would still be in our sins. Our faith would be foolish (1 Cor. 15:17). But Christ did rise, after that weekend of suffering and death, in a resurrection so glorious that those who lived through it would never want to erase it from their memories.

Even the risen Lord's appearances accented the new meaning of Sunday. On Easter Sunday He returned to the faithful in five separate incidents. One week later, also on a Sunday, He came to Thomas and showed him His wounded side. Seven Sundays later he poured out on them the Holy Spirit of Pentecost.

Sunday appears to be the day the Lord chose to be with His own in a special way; it was therefore also the obvious day when the disciples chose to be with their Lord. Was it any wonder that Sunday became a day such as the Sabbath had never been? Was it any wonder that the disciples instinctively chose Sunday as "the day of the Lord?" Was it any wonder that so many ancient writers of the church referred to Sunday as "little Easter"?

Among the disciples there seems to have been little difficulty about the choice of Sunday as *the* day of assembly. Even Peter, whose loyalty to the laws of Moses gave him many doubts of conscience over what he might eat and what he might not, appears to have had no problem with the choice of Sunday.

It was almost as if God Himself had selected Sunday. Therefore one cannot properly say that the *disciples* decided to replace the Sabbath—in their opinion *God* had already replaced it, as a symbol that He had set aside the Old Covenant and established the New.

What few references the New Testament provides all point to Sunday as the normal day of worship, whether recorded by Luke, Paul, or John. In Acts 20, for example, Luke writes of the visit to Troas and tells how Paul preached "upon the first day of the week, when the disciples came together to break bread." This is the famous service in which Eutychus fell asleep in the window and crashed to the street below.

This service was apparently held in a private house or apartment, on the third story of a tenement, not in a synagog, as was often the case. There were so many oil lamps that Luke makes a point of mentioning them (did they perhaps contribute to Eutychus' drowsiness?).

The apostle Paul everywhere seems to take it for granted that Sunday is the expected day of Christian worship. He exhorts the Corinthians to gather an offering for Jerusalem "upon *the first day of the week.*" He writes that he had given similar instructions to the churches in Galatia. St. John, in the Book of Revelation (1:10), terms Sunday the "Lord's Day" as if it were a matter of course.

The Days of the Week

The letters of Paul regularly refer to Sunday as "the first day of the week." By the time John is in exile on Patmos and is writing the Book of Revelation, the "first day" has assumed a new name—"the day of the Lord." The Greek word is *kyriake,* and means simply "the Lord's."

The Latin word is *dominicale* and has strongly influenced all the Romance tongues—those based on Latin. Even down to the 20th century we have such forms as *domingo* (Portuguese), *domenica*

(Italian), and *dimanche* (French). The other days of the week retained the names of Roman gods — Luna, Mars, Mercury, Jupiter, Venus, and Saturn.

In northern Europe the names of the days remained pagan, including even Sunday. Here the deities honored were the sun, the moon, Tiu, Woden, Thor, Freia, and Saturn — the last of course Roman. Early Christian writers like the Venerable Bede (673 – 735) suggest that the use of a pagan name ("Sun-day") was not a denial of one's faith but a kindly concession to those who had not yet come to know the Lord.

In a day when sending a letter to the farthest corner of the empire was a matter of months, there was little chance to make these names everywhere identical or to change them to Christian counterparts, for example, to the names of martyrs or apostles. This might have given all the lands of Christian Europe week days with similar names, like Peter day or Paul day or John day.

Such a renaming would have been visionary at any level, whether by emperor or pope, but one pope did suggest that the first day of the week be called "the Lord's Day," the last "the Sabbath," and all others simply bear a number, from second to sixth. This became the way to count the days of the week in medieval Latin. In Portuguese the names of the days still begin with *domingo,* continue from *segunda* through *sexta,* and end with *sabado.*

OTHER TIMES OF ASSEMBLY

Our Lord and His disciples had of course inherited the weekly pattern of their worship from their Jewish forebears, and much of this carried over into the new church. In the Jewish calendar the most important unit was the week, and the cornerstone of the week was the Sabbath.

The Jewish calendar was lunar, based on the 28-day cycle of the moon, with a 13th month to fill up the slack and make the cycles of the moon dovetail with those of the sun. In deference to the story of creation, the Jewish week consisted of seven days — six on which the Lord worked and one on which He rested.

In other cultures of that day the concept of a 7-day week was not so thoroughly established. The Greek week varied from three days to ten. The Roman one normally consisted of eight.

For the Jew the most sacred day of the week was the last — the Sabbath. Other days which the pious Hebrew marked as fast days, either at home or in the synagog, were Tuesday and Thursday. The

4

Christian purposely selected other days as fast days—Wednesday and Friday—but kept the basic Jewish pattern.

Nearly two thousand years later we can still see traces of this pattern in the Roman Catholic custom of holding special masses on the first Friday, or of abstaining from meat then, or in the Lutheran or Episcopalian habit of attending Lenten services on Wednesdays.

At first the Wednesday and Friday services were mere devotions, with the congregation standing (hence the word "station" or Station Days). By the fifth century the service regularly included a mass. Just as Sunday symbolized Christ's resurrection, Friday recalled His crucifixion, and Wednesday the day on which Judas had agreed to betray Him.

The Octave

Another Hebrew influence was the octave. The three great festivals of the Old Covenant were the Passover, Pentecost, and Tabernacles, and all three were celebrated not on a single day but for a whole week. "Seven days shall ye eat unleavened bread," God had instructed his people in Egypt (Ex. 12:15).

In the first century or two, with persecution and martyrdom rife, the young church had little opportunity to develop the major Christian festivals into octaves. Besides, Sunday was normally a workday, and worshiping eight days in a row presented some very real problems, especially when one's employers were not kindly disposed toward Christians. After the edict of Constantine in 313, however, major holy days did gradually begin to develop octaves, especially Easter, Christmas, and Pentecost.

All kinds of mystic symbolism gathered round the word octave, and Irenaeus devoted a whole book to the subject, *The Ogdoad,* unfortunately lost. When God had spoken to the people of Israel through Isaiah (1:13) about His annoyance with their new moons and sabbaths, their incense and their holy days, He promised that He would establish a great new kingdom of Zion, a great new "eighth day"—and this was what led to much of the speculation.

The Nature of Sunday

Originally Sunday was a day of joy, even as a workday. It was not a day of rest, as the Jewish Sabbath had been. It was not a day when one refrained from pleasure or business. Sunday was primarily a day when one celebrated Christ's resurrection and abiding presence.

As such it was not a fast day, not even in Lent. In the ancient church the faithful often knelt on weekdays but not on Sundays. Kneeling was a sign of penitence, the sign of humility a slave owed his master, totally foreign to the mood of Sunday or the relationship of a Christian to Christ.

This distinction the churches of the East have faithfully preserved. In the West, kneeling became more and more common, though one sign of change, especially in the Roman Catholic Church, is the rediscovered accent on standing. Even the host of the mass should now be received as the communicant *stands,* if the construction of the chancel and the altar rail allow, according to a decision of Vatican II.

Not until emperors officially took over the leadership in Christianity did the notions of the Hebrew Sabbath begin to creep into the observance of the Christian Sunday. The early fathers in fact feared that a day of rest would create more temptation and laziness than a good Christian should be exposed to. The normal view was that a man should first celebrate the Eucharist and then go about his work, knowing that the Sabbath of the Old Covenant was entirely different from the "Lord's Day" of the New.

Only under Constantine did laws begin to consider the possibility of closing down shops and taverns. Until well into the sixth century, the Christian farmer who had fulfilled his duty at church on Sunday was encouraged to resume his work of harvesting or planting.

In the reign of Gregory the Great (590 – 604), however, especially in the West, the church began to discourage the kind of work it called "servile," and urged instead that the whole day be given over to meditation, to pilgrimages, and to works of charity.

The wave of Puritanism that sprang up as a byproduct of the Reformation, especially in England, Scotland, and the Low Countries, gave a completely foreign flavor to Sunday. Even its name often changed from Sunday to "the Sabbath," and the ancient laws of the Jews, many of them Pharisaic rather than Mosaic, severely restricted what one could do and how he could worship. In America the Puritan observance of Sunday grew so severe that parents who allowed their children to play or even to read a nonreligious book were punished – a rather odd turn for a day which by its very origin was one of joy.

The Primacy of Easter

Just as the first Easter set the pattern for Sunday, so it also set the pattern for the church year. An event of such significance as the Resurrection soon formed a natural focus for the entire year. No wonder one of the church fathers called it the festival of all festivals – the *festum festorum.*

Easter was considered so important, in fact, that the church almost at once began to look forward to its coming and backward to its passing.

From this developed the pre-Easter and post-Easter seasons, better known as Lent and Pentecost.

Though the whole year pivoted around Easter, no one quite agreed when that first Easter had occurred or even when it should be celebrated. At first this made little difference—as Origen put it, the Christian who lives out each day in the presence of Christ, his true Paschal Lamb, celebrates Easter every day.

Christ Himself apparently had little desire to set up specific days to commemorate the various events in His life, but humans being humans, this was a natural and honest way to do Him honor. Thus Easter and in fact all the holy days were not divinely ordained but the result of human judgment and experience.

The Paschal, or Easter, festival was doubtless the earliest and the most important of all church celebrations, and at the same time the most controversial. Because it recalled at once Christ's last supper, His sacrifice *and* resurrection, one of the points at issue was how it was related to the original Passover.

Christians of strong Hebrew orientation preferred the same pattern the Jews had observed. This put Passover on the 14th day of the month of Nisan, regardless of the day of the week. Other Christians felt that since it was Christ's resurrection that formed the focus of the celebration, it should always fall on a Sunday, the original day of the Resurrection, regardless of the day of the month.

The Christians of Asia Minor who fought for the Hebrew pattern were called *Quartodecimani*—"Fourteeners". Western Christians, however, led by the bishop of Rome, argued that the whole pattern of commemorating the Resurrection Sunday after Sunday simply was not logical if Easter itself were allowed to fall on a Tuesday or Thursday or Saturday.

Epiphanius (315?—402), the metropolitan of Cyprus, sums up some of these differences of opinion vividly in these words: "Some began the festival before the week, some after the week, some at the beginning, some at the middle, some at the end, thus creating an amazing and troublesome confusion."

In 155, Polycarp, bishop of Smyrna in Asia Minor, journeyed to Rome to try to persuade Anicetus to reconsider the Quartodeciman point of view. Half a century later, Victor, who then held the chair of Peter, felt so strongly about the issue that he excommunicated an aged metropolitan of Ephesus solely over the date of Easter.

By the time of the Council of Nicaea in 325, which had as one of its tasks the proper dating of Easter, even the majority of Eastern bishops voted with the West, and the Easter-on-Sunday party won an easy, if still controversial, victory.

Unfortunately the bishops at Nicaea did not foresee another problem: how to determine the Sunday in question, that is, the proper way of calculating the Paschal full moon, which determined the dating of the Passover. The man who was most frequently consulted by Western Christians was the bishop of Alexandria, the center of astronomical studies.

Partly because of calendar reforms in 457 and in 525, and partly because there were various methods of calculating the Sunday after the Passover, Easter continued to be celebrated on as many as four or five different Sundays, depending on where one lived. The Venerable Bede (d. 735) tells how the King of Northumbria celebrated the feast of Easter while his poor queen, who had grown up accustomed to the Roman use, was still on the fast of Palm Sunday.

Religious conviction being what it is, missionary lands like England out at the fringes of Christendom were still split over the controversy as late as the seventh century. If the Council of Whitby in 664 accomplished little else, at least it brought the date of Easter in England in line with that of Rome. In certain remote backwashes of Christendom such as the Coptic and Syriac churches the issue is still a live one even in the 20th century.

THE MARTYRS

Of the many elements which helped shape the church's pattern of worship — the first day of the week, Easter, and the Jewish festivals — one is too often forgotten: the days of the martyrs. Persecution and martyrdom was the most massive test the young church had to face, and as the Roman authorities discovered, the blood of the martyrs really was the seed of the church.

From the time of the apostles until the time of Constantine, for nearly three centuries, Christians were subject to search and seizure anywhere, though most frequently when they came together for common worship. Ostensibly because they refused to worship the emperor, they were considered disloyal to the state and were therefore hounded from province to province.

Tertullian complains that a favorite trick of the police was to round them up in the midst of their public worship, off in a cave or catacomb or cemetery, sometimes in the dead of night. And yet these faithful believers did not give up "the assembling of themselves together," despite the threat of destruction, for as they shared a common loaf and a common cup, they were assuring themselves of Christ's presence.

8

"Where two or three are gathered together in My name, there am I in the midst of them." (Matt. 18:20)

This kind of loyalty was contagious. By his death a man could make telling witness. Under Roman law, no one could be buried within the city limits, and the bodies of the martyrs therefore rested outside the walls. Each year the faithful gathered at the martyr's tomb, usually on the anniversary of his death, to recall how great his faith had been—a "recollection," as they called it.

To the ancient church the day of a Christian's death and his heavenly birthday was far more important than the day of his earthly birth. This also helps to explain why the early Christians could celebrate Christ's death and resurrection long before they ever thought of celebrating his birth.

In general, saints and martyrs were celebrated only locally—even famous ones like James (Jerusalem) or Philip (Alexandria) or Peter (Rome). Seldom did the fame of any martyr, even of Peter or Paul, extend more than a hundred miles from where he had been buried.

After the time of the persecutions the body was often moved to a church, or a basilica was built over the grave. But during the first three centuries, even though the local ceremonies at the tomb may have been second only to Easter and Pentecost, the martyr was often unheard of even in the neighboring province.

The Pagan Influences

Just as the Christian world had adapted certain of its holy days from the people of Israel (Easter from Passover, and Pentecost from the Feast of Weeks), so it also had to confront the festivals of the pagan world. At first the faithful were so concerned with being distinct and separate from the rest of society that there was little concern for secular holidays, whether Greek, Roman, or Asiatic.

Yet as the church gradually opened its doors to the masses and faced the difficult problem of educating them, without printing presses or any system of compulsory schooling, it naturally started to replace the pagan festivals with Christian ones. Often as not it retained the pagan name but sought to change the character of the original feast, as, for example, when the old midwinter festival of the returning sun became the Christian Christmas, the birthday of the Eternal Sun.

Pope Gregory I (540—604) openly championed this procedure. First win men's confidence, not their enmity, and gradually begin to educate them, he argued. Non-Christian temples were not to be destroyed; they were to become Christian houses of worship. Nordic festivals were not to be condemned; they were to be Christianized.

Pagan names were not to be discarded; they were to be filled with Christian meaning. This is in fact exactly how we got the English name for Easter, or for that matter, Sun-Day.

Naturally the long centuries of transition from a church of the catacombs to a church of the empire, though already a decaying empire, were confused ones, especially in the West, where the political upheavals were worse than in the East. But even in the East golden-voiced John Chrysostom, the Patriarch of Constantinople, had good reason to complain of all the confusion he saw. In one of his sermons he laments that although the faithful are eager to celebrate all kinds of festivals, in fact whatever the bishops suggest, for the most part they have not the slightest notion what they are celebrating.

When being a Christian became not only safe but fashionable, the church developed new interests in elaborate ceremony and ritual. Christian celebration was no longer a secret affair in a barn or catacomb. Now it strove to be distinctive, with new rites, processions, garb, and ceremony, paralleling the glory of the imperial court.

In the mosaics and frescoes Christ was now depicted as the great Pantocrator, the Ruler of the universe, Christ the King. The church's public worship was seen as the earthly counterpart to the glory of the heavenly court. Instead of focusing on the present reality of Christ's redemptive victory and on our participating in it here and now, the church's various celebrations were becoming a historical kind of *memorial.*

In the church of the earlier days Christ had been thought of primarily as *present.* Every Sunday was a "little Easter". The normal Sunday service, the Eucharist, was a symbolic reliving of Christ's *total* redemptive triumph, recalling and making present "all that our Lord had done for us." The Christian was made a partaker of Christ's death and resurrection in baptism and was renewed and nurtured by it in the week-by-week communion. There was no need to have a separate Good Friday and Easter, or Ascension and Pentecost, since all these events were a present reality.

But now the mentality began to change. Now Christianity was big business. Now the pagan masses pouring into the church could not be properly catechized nor be expected to know what the new life in Christ was all about. They were primarily spectators, not participants in the "holy mysteries," the sacraments. Therefore there was a new accent in the services on the events of the gospels, on Christian teaching, and on Christian celebration. The idea of historical anniversaries and of a systematic recalling of the fundamentals of the faith was introduced. This can best be seen in the development of the two halves of the church year, one accenting the major events in Christ's life and the other His role as teacher and example.

THE IMPORTANCE OF JERUSALEM

Helena, Emperor Constantine's mother, is a good example of the new outlook. With her gold and her zeal, the faithful at Jerusalem began to seek out those sites closely associated with the life of Christ — where He was buried, where He was crucified, where He was born. Great basilicas began to spring up, and there was a renewed interest in searching for relics, whether of Christ, the apostles, or the martyrs.

Throngs of pilgrims began to make their way toward Jerusalem — nobles, bishops, kings, even the poor and lowly. What they discovered there was not merely the place where Jesus had lived but a great and thriving church, and one which had developed a complex pattern of rites and ceremonies connected with the life of the Savior. From these rites much of the church year has developed.

One such pilgrim was an adventurous lady from Spain, perhaps the abbess of a convent, variously called Silvia or Etheria. Silvia journeyed to Jerusalem in the 380s or 390s and kept a diary of what she found there. This *Pilgrimage of Silvia* gives the first and most detailed picture of the church year.

The major festival about which Silvia writes, as we would expect, is Easter. In the three centuries since the death of the apostles Easter had developed the kind of ritual and splendor one would expect in the Near East, with glorious chants, pantomimes, readings, prayers, pennons, and processions.

Already at the time of Silvia most of the holy days we now consider important were in existence in Jerusalem. Christmas was the only major exception. The rest were already going strong — Epiphany (which dealt in the Christian East not with the Magi and Christ's appearance to the Gentiles, but with His birth and baptism), the Presentation, Palm Sunday, Maundy Thursday, Good Friday, Holy Saturday, Easter, the octave of Easter, and finally Pentecost, which in Silvia's account was a joint celebration with Ascension.

What makes Silvia's diary of unusual value is her keen eye for detail and her realistic description of the rites and services in which she took part. She writes of the wondrous church life in Jerusalem as if it were far more organized than what she had known in Spain. Doubtless it was pilgrims of her status and enthusiasm who helped spread the whole idea of the church year from Jerusalem to the West.

This is not to say that the festivals which Silvia mentions were celebrated only at Jerusalem. Doubtless they were kept with equal

11

fervor at Antioch, Constantinople, and Alexandria. Yet the fact that they were customary at Jerusalem gave them a sacred prestige, since they came from the land where the sacred events had actually taken place.

Thus by the end of the fourth century the church year had assumed a form we would recognize today. Christmas, of course, still had considerable growing to do, and Lent and Advent were little more than unsprouted seeds. Yet the outline was all there.

2
The Year and the Liturgy

WORSHIP AND LITURGY

The whole life of the Christian is an act of worship, in the New Testament sense — *latreia*. Worship is not merely what one does on Sunday morning or before meals or before going to bed. It involves every hour of every day of every year. Thus Luther can properly speak of the Virgin Mary "worshiping" when she is mopping the floor, dusting the stove, or washing diapers.

In the more usual meaning worship refers to the public act of Christians who have come together for praise, confession, absolution, intercession, offering of selves, and celebrating the Sacrament — expressed in various traditions within Christendom in such phrases as "the service," morning prayer, common prayer, public worship, Holy Communion, mass, or the divine liturgy.

To a degree even those churches which pride themselves in having no liturgy at all make of public worship something liturgical — invocation, lections, offering, instruction, communal singing, Baptism and the Lord's Supper. They, too, have a considerable heritage from the Hebrews and the early Christians, even though they may not be aware of it.

Strictly, the growth and development of the order of common worship is a subject all its own, like church architecture or hymnody, but one cannot completely overlook it in a study of the church year without losing perspective. How the Easter vigil differed from the ordinary mass or how both differed from the litany of a Rogation day means nothing unless one knows something at least of the normal order.

The word liturgy comes from two Greek words and refers to "people" and to a "public work." If a Greek gave a banquet for his village or built a well at the crossroads, he was performing a *leitourgia*, an act for the common good. In the New Testament the word comes to be reserved for conducting divine worship — as in Acts 13:2.

The Eastern Orthodox churches quite properly call their service the divine liturgy—an excellent choice, not only because it is historic but also because it involves the concept of a "people of God" *(laos theou)*, in the fine old sense of the Old Testament.

In the Western tradition, once Latin took the place of Greek in the liturgy, the technical word for the service was mass (Latin, *missa*), as we still find it in words like Christ*mas* or Candle*mas*. The word comes from the closing phrase in the service, *Ite, missa est,* which can variously be translated: "Go, it is over," "Go, you are dismissed," or "Go, you are sent forth."

Strictly speaking, mass means the dismissal or the benediction. Though mass eventually came to mean only the highest and most important of the orders of worship, or "offices," namely the Eucharist, for many centuries it referred to any kind of religious function where there was a benediction or blessing.

Even in a document late enough to describe Holy Week processions in Rome during the fifth and sixth centuries, the faithful are described as going to *missae* in a dozen different churches. Because of the time and the distance, full services could not possibly have been celebrated at each.

Ritual books from the seventh century continue to refer to the Matins "mass" *(missa matutina)* and Vespers "mass" *(missa nocturna)*, even though the Eucharist was not a part of those offices.

For one reason or another many Christians who are not Roman Catholic shy away from the word "mass," perhaps because of its later connotations of a repeating of Christ's sacrifice. Luther continued to use the term interchangeably with the Lord's Supper. The Augsburg Confession specifically sanctions the use of the word among Lutherans. Among Scandinavian Lutherans it was retained as the normal term for the Sunday service. Among the Anglicans Cranmer and his contemporaries also used it, though the Book of Common Prayer 20 years later seems to prefer the term Holy Communion.

But whatever its name, there can be no doubt about the nature of the one service that from the time of Christ Himself the early church upheld as the greatest honor they could offer to God, the office of the Eucharist. And this of course is so closely connected with the Passover meal that scholars ever since have been trying to split them apart.

THE PASSOVER

The Passover was primarily a family affair, not one of the synagog, not one which usually involved more than the immediate members of the family. Among the Jews, family worship had an old and established tradition, and the Pesach was among the oldest and the most honored of all the rites.

As the foods for the meal stood on the table, the lamb, the bitter herbs, the unleavened bread, and the wine, one of the children asked what these foods symbolized. The father then offered a prayer of thanksgiving, retold the story of the plagues, of the bondage, and of the exodus, and then led the group in singing the lesser Hallelujah, taken from Psalms 112 and 113.

Then the head of the house took the bread into his hands, blessed it, broke it, and gave it to all who were present. This was the real start of the dinner. Only after the meal was over did he fill the cup, bless it, and ceremoniously offer it to his household. As a closing prayer the family sang the greater Hallelujah, taken from Psalms 113, 117, 118, and 135.

THE INSTITUTION

This was probably the pattern our Lord followed with His disciples in the upper room — prayers, praises, the unleavened bread, the meal, instruction and conversation, and finally the cup of blessing. Luke and Paul seem to indicate that the bread was distributed before the meal, and the cup of blessing afterward, but Matthew and Mark are silent about the timing. Some scholars suggest that even in the evangelists' lifetime the church had begun to celebrate the Lord's Supper without an intervening meal.

THE EUCHARIST UNTIL CONSTANTINE

Three times in the book of Acts we find the phrase "the breaking of bread" without any mention of an intervening meal. In 1 Cor. 11:20, however, Paul indicates that there *was* a feast (the so-called love banquet or *agape*) in conjunction with the Lord's Supper and that for one reason or another (drunkenness, breaking into separate groups, bickering, not waiting for all to arrive, departures from the Lord's ordinances) Paul would need to reinstruct the Corinthians when he arrived.

Concerning the celebration of the Eucharist by the generation after the death of the disciples we know nothing, but by the middle of the second century we have several detailed descriptions of this rite, including religious ones like those in the *Didache* (supposedly a summary of apostolic teaching) and Justin Martyr's *Apology,* as well as a secular account by the historian Pliny the Younger.

By the year 150 the service is no longer held at sundown but early in the morning, usually before daybreak, in a private house, in a room that contains only the holy table and perhaps a few chairs for the clergy.

15

Usually the ruler or master of the feast was the bishop, though presbyters could substitute in his absence. The faithful brought their own bread and wine, and what was not used for the Holy Supper was later distributed to the poor. Singing, prayers, and responses were already known, though not formally fixed or required.

In the first two or three centuries the normal liturgy fell into distinct halves, known as the Mass of the Catechumens (those who were still taking instructions for membership and baptism) and the Mass of the Faithful. Other names for these are the Ante-Communion and the Communion, or the Office of the Word and the Office of the Sacrament.

Since the Eucharistic rite was too sacred and too secret (perhaps even too dangerous during the age of the persecutions) for those who were taking instructions but were not yet baptized, all but the faithful were cleared from the room for the second half of the service.

Thus did the early liturgies develop, with a considerable amount of cross-fertilization. Those in the East soon came to full flower, especially at Jerusalem and at Alexandria, and a bit later at Constantinople. Named after St. Mark, St. James, St. Basil, and St. Chrysostom, these do not differ significantly today from the form they had reached by the year 450.

The worship of the Eastern Church is marked by a childlike wonder and trust, with an awesome sense of God's majesty, and with dramatic symbols appealing to heart and hand—incense, ikons, elaborate garments, processions, and the like. An embassy sent by a prince of Kiev in the 10th century to study the worship of the Greeks reported that it had never seen such magnificent buildings, such splendor, such a sense of the indwelling of God. "We did not know," they reported, "whether we were in heaven or on earth. . . . We cannot forget the beauty."

THE SERVICE BOOKS AFTER CONSTANTINE

In the West, what information we can gather about the life and worship of the church of the Constantinian age comes from such books as sacramentaries, missals, and calendars. These give us a fairly good picture of the prayers, lessons, propers, and the ordinary, and an even better sense of the church year.

The sacramentaries which show us most about the life of the church are those that come from Rome, chiefly the Leonine, the Gelasian, and the Gregorian, dating variously from about 460 to 610. From these come a great bulk of the prayers and Scripture lessons still in use today, whether the church be Roman Catholic, Lutheran, or Anglican. Artistically, the Gregorian gives us a whole new insight into the use of the chant and of music in the service—the glories of Gregorian plainsong.

The rites and uses of which we know most, from historical documents and references, are the Syrian (St. James), the Egyptian (Saint Mark), the Nestorian, the Byzantine, the Ephesian (St. John), the Mozarabic (Spain), the Gallican (France), the Ambrosian (Milan), the Stowe (Irish), the Leofric (early English), the Sarum (Norman English), and the Roman (St. Peter).

These generally list the holy days for a specific time and place, give the wording of prayers, prescribe Scripture readings, and occasionally add rubrics—so-called because they were written in red ink *(rubrum)*—about what the priest is to do.

For at least the first four or five centuries the pope was considered *primus inter pares* ("first among equals"). Because of his primacy and that of Peter, one would expect that the Roman use would have quickly supplanted the others. Though considerable pressures were exerted in this direction by the more energetic of the popes, for example, Gregory the Great, the non-Roman liturgies actually had a long and flourishing life.

One advantage of so many different liturgies was the rich variety of worship. Yet suppression, improvements in travel and communication, and the passage of time caused some to fall by the wayside.

With many we can trace exactly how this happened—for example, how Rome suppressed the Gallican rite during the 9th century and the Mozarabic in the 11th. Even with forced conformity, however, the old liturgies died hard. Rich nobles, or perhaps even rich archbishops, as in Spain, set aside money and foundations to maintain the ancient and nationalistic liturgies within their own enclaves, even after Rome had ordered conformity.

When Charlemagne assumed the crown of the Holy Roman Empire in 800, one of his wisest decisions was to import Alcuin as his religious adviser. The English monk proved to be one of the best liturgists of the millenium; and the political stability of Charlemagne's reign gave continuity to his effort to unify the various traditions. The only fault of these Romano-Frankish sacramentaries is their tendency toward wordiness and florid speech and their multiplication of countless new prayers.

Generally, though, the effort to unify the various orders was necessary. Someone, somewhere, had to try to bring together these hundreds of rites, and the bishop of Rome deserves a measure of credit for attempting what at first must have seemed impossible—a reasonably common canon.

To speak of *one* liturgy or even of *one* church year, even by the time of St. Thomas Aquinas in the 13th century, would be rash. There was a standardized Roman rite, to be sure, but outside Rome it was adhered to more in the neglect than in the keeping. In Germany, for example, the missals popular among both priests and people were those of Bamberg, Mainz, and Augsburg.

England's famous Sarum use (Salisbury) set the pace not only for what was done throughout most of England but also for the other great seafaring nations — Holland, Sweden, Spain, and Portugal. Prince Henry the Navigator, an early contemporary of Columbus, much preferred the Sarum use to the Roman one and ordered it for the royal chapel.

Yet to claim that the liturgy of the church varied so distinctly from country to country that a traveler from England would not be able to follow a service in Italy or Germany would be to exaggerate the differences. The chief distinction was in the prefatory elements, stressing the sinner's penitence and God's forgiveness, along with the conclusion, the benediction, and the thanksgiving.

The main elements, including the *ordinary* (those parts which generally remained the same from service to service) and the *propers* (those which varied with each Sunday or season) were similar throughout the West. With some exceptions, these elements, along with the basic structure of the church year, still remain the liturgical heritage common to all the Western churches, especially the Roman Catholic, the Lutheran, and the Anglican.

To a varying degree they can be found even in the churches of a Reformed or Wesleyan tradition. Quite oddly, because of late additions to the Roman rite, many of the Lutheran and Anglican usages are closer to those of ancient Latin Christianity than those of Roman Catholicism, though Vatican II has already done much to hasten a return to the older and simpler pattern.

The Variables of the Service

After the Confession of Sins, or the preface, the service proper begins with the Introit. In Latin *introitus* signifies "entrance," and the term originally referred to the psalm verses sung at the time the priest entered the church and proceeded to the altar. It is a kind of gateway to the service proper. In spirit and in language the psalms which make up most of the Introits help carry out the mood of the day, whether it is joyous, sorrowful, meditative, or penitential.

The Gloria Patri, the Kyrie, and the Gloria in Excelsis (omitted during certain seasons) are all fixed parts of the ordinary. The Kyrie ("Lord, have mercy") is of Greek origin, as its name implies, and is one of the oldest elements of Christian worship, especially used in many of the litanies for processions.

Next comes the Collect. The Collect is the prayer appointed for a particular day. Some authorities think the word originates from the group of deacons who had assembled, or "collected," for this prayer; others think it more likely that the Collect was originally a bidding prayer, made up of the requests of many different people, "collected" and condensed into the common petition.

Whatever its origin, the Collect remains one of the most meaningful elements of the liturgy. Polished and jewel-like, its crisp words present the needs and conditions of Christians who lived 1400 or 1500 years ago, often when their churches and towns were being invaded and burned. It belongs to the heritage that Christians have faithfully passed from generation to generation. Cranmer's translations and revisions in the Book of Common Prayer have made them a treasure in English even to those who know no Latin.

After the Collect come the Lessons. The customs concerning these readings from Scriptures are among the oldest in Christianity and recall how Christ Himself stood up in the synagog and read from the Prophets. The Jews divided the Old Testament into three sections, the Law, the Prophets, and the Writings, and read from each section, often with an interpretation or homily.

The early Christians continued this use of the Old Testament, besides using the New. In the first four centuries they read at least five (and perhaps as many as eight) separate categories of sacred writings. The most frequent were the Law, the Prophets, the Epistles, the Acts, and the Gospels.

By the fifth century they cut the number of readings to three: the Old Testament, the Epistles, and the Gospels. By the seventh century the reading of the Old Testament in the service was usually bypassed, except on festivals or at Matins or Vespers. Since Vatican II the Roman use is restoring the Old Testament lessons, as do many of the lectionaries of the Reformation.

Collectively the Scripture readings were known as pericopes, a Greek word that means cut, slice, section, or selection. Epistles and Gospels were normally copied into separate books with elaborate bindings and read by separate lectors or deacons from separate parts of the chancel.

Traditionally the altar stood in the east end of the church, with the worshipers in the west, facing the rising sun, a symbol of the Christ who was the Light of the world. In these terms the Epistle was read from a desk or ambo on the south side of the chancel, or in smaller churches, from the south "horn" of the altar. The Gospel was read from the north position, or from the people's left.

Just how and why the specific readings were selected for a given Sunday is not very clear. Few seem to have any connection with the church year, a good indication that they were established very early, before there was a year. Some may have come from the ancient practice of *lectio continua,* in which a whole book was read in sequence.

The ancient church held the system of appointed readings so sacred it hesitated to make changes even though the church year changed. The church of the Reformation advocated varying sets of pericopes, to cover a larger part of the Scriptures, a practice that is now winning favor also in Roman Catholic circles.

Often the Epistle was read by a lector, or even by a distinguished layman, as has for centuries been the custom in the Church of England, or as the Roman Catholic Church is again doing. The Gospel was considered especially sacred, and the book in which the lessons were inscribed was often bound in the finest leather, embellished with gold leaf and jewels, with the verses drawn in purple ink and the capitals in gold. An elaborate ceremony for reading the Gospel, still common in the Orthodox churches, included the ceremonial kiss, the ritual censing, and the solemn procession to carry it to the ambo.

Since the Epistle and the Gospel were read from opposite sides of the chancel, the versicle which covered the time lag while the officiants moved from one position to another was called the Gradual. A *gradus* is a step or incline, and may be evidence that the stand from which the Gospel was read was higher than the one for the Epistle. It could of course also refer to the altar steps from which the verses were sung. Luther was especially fond of the Gradual. The great Hallelujah always reminded him of choirs of angels.

The Reformation and the American Development

Generally the Lutheran reformers retained nearly all of the Western liturgy. What they discarded was certain practices and prayers in the fixed part of the canon which, they thought, obscured the unique sacrifice of Christ on the cross.

In reforming the liturgy Luther was conservative. He attempted to save everything which did not appear contrary to Scripture, especially those elements which made faith tangible and which seemed to have been the practice of the apostolic church.

Zwingli at first followed the pattern of Luther, though he was later to cut the liturgy drastically. Calvin attempted to eradicate any liturgy he could not find in the Scriptures or in the early church, and his even more drastic followers soon turned the house of God into a barren hall, without pictures, statues, altar, or even, for a time, a cross.

In England the first Book of Common Prayer borrowed heavily from the Lutheran orders, with additional prayers from the Eastern Orthodox rites. Cranmer, its gifted editor, had spent a year and a half in Germany, studying the Lutheran forms, and had married the niece of Osiander, one of the leading Lutheran liturgists. This, plus more than 20 years of practical experience with the German order, helped make the English prayer book the outstanding book it is.

With the great religious tidal wave that had swept out of Wittenberg and Geneva and Canterbury, leaders in the Roman Catholic Church also took a hard look at the liturgy. At the Council of Trent (1545−63) a special commission was charged with examining the *abusus missae*, "the abuses of the mass."

It discussed, among many other items, the almost superstitious reverence for the corporal (the cloth on which the sacred vessels are placed); the great multiplication of side altars, sometimes as many as 40 or 50; the growth of private or votive masses without a congregation, especially those said for the dead; the concept of merely being present or watching the mass, without taking part; the recitation of the rosary or other private devotions during mass.

Berthold of Chiemsee, writing in 1528, indicates that the spirit of reform strongly influenced even such staunch citadels of the faith as Salzburg. There, he records, the archbishop had once been able to maintain more than a hundred *gratiani* (priests who did not serve a parish but offered private masses for the dead in exchange for a fee). Now Luther's theology had so dammed up the flow of stipends that the archbishop could no longer support even one.

Reformers of all varieties also downgraded the medieval emphasis on saints. Except for the Evangelists, apostles, and perhaps a dozen others, the saints were generally ignored, perhaps too much so, a natural reaction to the proliferation of saints' days to a point where the Christ-centered nature of the church year was neglected. Besides, both civil and church authoritites had for centuries objected to a calendar in which there were more days of idleness than of work, more holy days than ordinary ones.

Among some of the Reformed groups, and especially among the Puritans, the mere mention of a saint's day or even of the church calendar smacked of "popery." Church statuary or woodcarving or stained glass, especially if it portrayed the Virgin or the saints, fell before the ax and the hammer. Since this was the era when the New World was being colonized, worship in America generally had a strong anti-Catholic and antiliturgical atmosphere, and influenced even the liturgical churches toward a nonliturgical pattern.

In 1689, for example, when the royal governor of Massachusetts tried to introduce the Book of Common Prayer there, he ran up against a stone wall. Increase Mather, Boston's leading divine, called liturgical services "sinful" and said the rites of the prayer book were "broken responds and shreds of prayer which the priests and people toss between them like tennis balls."

After the colonial days, when the westward expansion was in full bloom, the kind of religion most popular between the seaboard and the frontier was that of the camp meeting — an informal kind of service that people could indulge in out of doors, in their cabins, or in little clapboard churches. These were occasional gatherings of settlers who came from a wide area whenever an itinerant preacher came by.

In the 20th century, however, the churches are once again discovering the value of the church year and of the liturgy. A new Methodist or Presbyterian church, complete with altar, lectern, and chancel, is often indistinguishable from a Lutheran or Episcopal one.

In the absence of a church year, the American search for something to celebrate, in distinct contrast to the attitude of the old New Englanders who thought it sinful even to exchange wedding rings or to sing Christmas carols, has led to some rather unusual and nonliturgical Sundays: Rally Day, Mission Sunday, Mother's Day, Rural Life Sunday, World Communion Day, and World Day of Prayer. Even if these are a giant step away from the tradition of the historic church, at least they show that worshipers everywhere seek some kind of emphasis, variety, and festivity when it is otherwise missing.

3

Vestments, Colors, and Customs

ADAPTATION AND CHANGE

The growth of the Christian year was largely accidental, despite the fact that it was based on the primacy of Sunday and of Easter. Since God has a hand in all history, however, He made use of these "accidents" to help man worship Him in a meaningful way.

That Christ died on a Friday and rose on a Sunday, for example, was incidental. The events would have been just as meaningful if they had occurred on a Tuesday and a Thursday. But once they had happened, the church settled on these days and invested them with special meaning.

Many other things in the church's life seem equally incidental— what kind of buildings it worshiped in, what kind of liturgy it developed, what kind of garb its priests wore, what date it chose for Christmas, what it demanded of the faithful, what it could do to win the barbarian. Its method was one of trial and error, adaptation to the needs of society, and borrowing and imitation.

Sometimes one development collided head-on with another. For example, the church made Christmas coincide with the Roman Saturnalia and thereby had to discard or move saints' days that stood in the way. When the season of Lent became strongly penitential, it adapted even the Sunday propers (except the Lessons) to the new mood of sorrow and meditation.

Fasting on Sunday was long considered inappropriate. By the Middle Ages, however, fasting before Communion had become an every-Sunday normality. Among the early Christians the church year influenced even the posture one assumed. Though kneeling and lying prostrate were in some communities considered appropriate on weekdays, they were considered wrong on Sunday, which was the joyous feast of Christ's resurrection.

Generally the church year was closely tied to church garb and custom. For example, the question of what color a priest wore when he was conducting a service might at first seem to have little to do with worship or the calendar. By the time of Aquinas, however, in the West liturgical colors begin to be tied to the seasons.

In the first centuries, when services were conducted largely in private dwellings, the priest seems to have worn ordinary clothing. After the persecutions churchgoers and priests alike tended to wear their best possible clothing as a special honor to the Lord.

In origin the vestments for the Eucharist were not special garments but what any well-dressed man would wear. Not until the time of Charlemagne did the officiant begin to look significantly different from those he led in worship.

In fact, the attitude toward garb seems to have been one of disinterest. What one wore, according to the church fathers, was one's own business, provided he did not let it stand in the way of his service to his people.

About the year 430 Celestine I bitterly scathed two bishops in southern France for being too much interested in garb. He wrote: "We churchmen should be distinguished by our learning, not our dress; by our habit of life, not by our clothing; by the purity of our minds, not by the cut of our garments."

In the centuries after the fall of the Roman Empire, the church seems to have considered itself the guardian not only of things spiritual but also, to a degree, of things cultural—to uphold classical Roman dress. The writers of this period quote chapter and verse on the symbolic and holy meaning of the tunic and mantle.

In the ninth century Spain and France, the elder daughters of the church, developed a differing style of chasuble and alb. Not oddly, perhaps, exactly the same thing was happening at the same time in the field of the liturgy. During the Crusades differences of opinion about garb became more animated. Some churchmen insisted that a bishop should be the most richly dressed man in the diocese; others felt he should wear the simple clothes of a John the Baptist.

After the Normans had invaded England in 1066, such head-on confrontations were common between the fancy Normans and the plain Saxons. The English were accustomed to a simpler style of dress, with no rich brocades or costly furs or jeweled copes, whereas the Normans were among the best-dressed bishops anywhere.

Wulfstan, a saintly old bishop of Worcester, made himself a hero when he resisted pressures from the Normans to dress more lavishly. When his superior advised him to wear richer garb—for example, the more stylish cat's fur instead of plain lamb's wool—Wulfstan pointed out that the liturgy he used made frequent mention of the "Lamb of God" but none at all of the "Cat of God."

At the time of the Reformation there was at least a reasonable conformity in many parts of Europe in the kind of garb worn by the parish priest. His major garments included the black cassock, the white alb, and the colored chasuble.

He usually wore such lesser paraphernalia as the stole (about the neck), the maniple (over the wrist), and the amice (over the shoulders). Every one of these vestments had symbolic ties with doctrine and history, was put on with a special prayer, and in the eyes of the common people was a kind of mystic link with the church of Peter and Paul, even though Peter and Paul might not have recognized these garments in their new shapes and materials.

Because of the religious asceticism of the more radical reformers of the 16th century, the vestments were among the first items called into question. Luther, on the contrary, argued that all vestments were adiaphora—that is, that they did not really matter, one way or the other. Therefore the old garb was often retained among the Lutherans, except perhaps for the too elaborate vestments of the bishops, such as copes and rochets.

Over the centuries, at least until recently, the chasuble and the alb have largely disappeared from Lutheran churches, except in Scandinavia—perhaps because of the wave of Pietism that swept Europe and America in the 1700s. The tight-fitting black cassock often became a flowing black robe and the only garb worn by the officiating pastor. In Scandinavia the common practice both at the time of the Reformation and now is to wear at least the alb with stole for the liturgy and the cassock with white bands for preaching. The chasuble never completely disappeared, and even where it has not been generally used for generations it is now being reintroduced for the celebration of the Eucharist.

In Geneva, Calvin contended that vestments had no Scriptural basis and were too deeply enmeshed in superstitious piety and the pomp of the Roman Church. For these reasons he argued for a complete ban. In the early reforms at Geneva there even seems to have been some resentment against the use of the black loose-fitting robe, similar to that which many Americans know as the "Geneva gown."

Perhaps because of the close ties of Calvin and the university, the academically styled gown, together with the white bands worn not only by clergymen but also by lawyers, judges, professors, or beadles, soon came to be the standard dress of many a Reformed dominie and perhaps the most common garb of American clergymen.

In England the ebb and flow of politics and reformation confused the picture. At first Anglican garb retained the black cassock for preaching and the white alb and the colored chasuble for the Eucharist. The second Book of Common Prayer, however, specified a compromise position between traditionalists and Puritans, requiring a white surplice over the black cassock and banning the fancier chasuble.

This was somewhat of an odd turn because the surplice had never really been a commonly used vestment, except for subdeacons and servers and minor clergy or for non-Eucharistic services. Yet since many worshipers felt that the chasuble was intimately connected with the sacrifice of the mass and was far too elaborate, the English reformers generally discouraged its use. In America many Lutherans borrowed the garb of the second prayer book—cassock, surplice, and stole—though the Lutheran surplice was somewhat longer than the Anglican.

The clerical collar, jokingly known as the dog collar, is one of the innovations of the last century. Among the Cavaliers of the 17th century it had been a broad collar lying flat, somewhat like a Buster Brown collar. Later, only the wings or bands were retained, a form that was common in the American pulpit two generations ago and in Europe four or five generations ago. In France, especially in Protestant areas, such bands are still worn by the clergy, though black, recalling the period of mourning for Louis XIV. Eventually even these bands disappeared, leaving only a close-fitting circle.

LITURGICAL COLORS

At first the color of the vestments seems to have been immaterial. The first official mention of liturgical colors occurs in an edict of Innocent III, who assumed the chair of Peter in 1198. Not till Pius V in 1572 was there any kind of binding force about liturgical colors—half a century after the time of the Reformation.

Liturgical colors as we know them today seem to have originated out of the mystical meanings of color during the Crusades. In the East the full range and development of color has been even more recent than in the West, and many a Balkan village still relies largely on white and red.

White and red seem to have remained especially popular also in certain parts of the West. In England the Sarum use, one of the most distinguished and longest-lived of Western rites, required only these two colors.

The four colors we know most commonly today were all reasonably well established by the time of the Reformation: green, red, violet, and white. Black and rose were also sufficiently frequent to be adopted into the Roman canon. Popular variants in Germany included yellow, gray, and scarlet, and in England blue and yellow. In fact, blue and yellow were hardest to suppress and in England have never wholly disappeared. The English Book of Common Prayer is wholly silent on the question of liturgical colors.

Nowadays most Western churches that use liturgical colors at all follow the pattern ordered for the Latin rite by Pius V. Churches that adhere to the general sequence of these colors include the Lutheran and the Anglican and even some nonliturgical ones like the Presbyterian and Methodist.

According to the Latin pattern, white is used from Christmas through the octave of Epiphany, from Easter Eve to the Eve of Whitsunday, for Trinity, for the other festivals of Christ, for the festivals of the Virgin Mary, for All Saints' Day, for the festivals of saints not martyrs, for the festivals of angels, for the Nativity of John the Baptist, for the Chair of St. Peter, for the Day of St. John Apostle and Evangelist, for the Conversion of Paul, and for such other ceremonies as the consecration of churches, the election of bishops, for weddings, baptisms, and children's funerals.

Red is used for Whitsunday and its octave (though Whitsunday in English means "white Sunday"), for the discovery of the cross, for the days of all apostles except those cited for white, for all martyrs, and for Holy Innocents (if on Sunday).

Green is used from the octave of Epiphany to Septuagesima and from Trinity Monday till Advent, except for intervening holidays.

Violet is used for Advent, for the Lenten and pre-Lenten period (Septuagesima to Maundy Thursday), and for Ember days. In the Roman rite it is also used for rituals involving the forgiveness of sins, such as the first part of the rite of baptism, the entire rite of confession, exorcism, and the anointing of the sick.

Lesser colors include black, for Good Friday and funerals, and rose, for the third Sunday in Advent and the fourth in Lent. Cloth of gold was a frequent substitute for red, white, or green, and cloth of silver for white.

In general, Western churches other than the Roman retain the colors of the season regardless of the rite. At a baptism in Lent, for example, the paraments would remain violet and at a funeral during the Trinity season they would remain green.

The Ember days were once days when Roman farmers paraded through their pastures and fields, to ask the gods' blessings, especially at the time of sowing, harvesting, and grape-picking. A similar pattern had been known in the Old Testament, and in fact in many places along the Mediterranean.

The first Christian Embertide dates from Callistus, about 222. Then, while the Roman world was feasting and dancing, the Christians were fasting and praying. By the fourth century the Embertides were celebrated four times a year, with special rites on the Wednesday, Friday, and Saturday of Ember weeks. They soon came to be popular for the ordination of priests, for fairs, tournaments, court sessions, school terms, and rent periods.

This was also the time when the faithful were encouraged to commune, especially after the 14th and 15th centuries. For many centuries the mass had been wrongly regarded as something to be watched, not something to be shared in. Thus Luther was advocating nothing new when he wrote that the faithful should commune at least four times a year—he was trying to persuade the people to return to the early-Christian practice of frequent communion, and was citing the four seasons of the Embertide as an absolute minimum.

The Gospels for the Ember days deal almost exclusively with exorcism and with demons. *Ember* itself comes from a word meaning seasons. Since the time of Gregory VII (1020?—1085) the Ember days fall in the week of the third Sunday in Advent, the first Sunday in Lent, during Pentecost week, and the week after the Exaltation of the Cross (September 14). An old English rhyme helped school children remember:

> Fasting days and Emberings be
> Lent, Whitsun, Holyrood, and Lucie.

ROGATION DAYS

"The three Rogation Days," says the Book of Common Prayer, are "the Monday, Tuesday, and Wednesday before Holy Thursday, or the Ascension of our Lord." Like the Ember days, they developed from pagan processions round the city, with chants and responses to frighten away demons.

The word *rogare* means to ask, to beseech, as in one of the common responses made by the people as they marched along: "We beseech Thee to hear us, good Lord." Rogationtide seems to have originated in 5th-century France at a time of great floods. The custom was not adopted at Rome for more than 300 years, chiefly because it fell in the midst of the great Fifty Days after Easter and thus interfered with the joyous mood of the Resurrection.

The chants and responses by the clergy and the people came to be called litanies, and the word *litania* frequently came to mean the procession itself. The *Kyrie eleison* ("Lord, have mercy") was chanted along the route. In Germany any religious song sung while traveling came to be known as a *Kyrieleis* or simply a *Leis* or *Lei,* perhaps by folk etymology related to the English word *lay,* meaning a song or poem.

Other Customs

The mixing of what was heathen and what was Christian often led to misunderstandings. In the second century classical writers accused the Christians of being sun worshipers because with some consistency they built their altars toward the east. The truth was that this was a natural borrowing from the Jews, who turned toward Jerusalem when they said their prayers.

Generally the Christians did build their churches with the altar toward the east, or more properly, toward Jerusalem. In those parts of the early church that lay east of Jerusalem, such as India and Syria, there are not enough archaeological remains to generalize, though here the orientation (a word which means eastward-facing) probably symbolized the greatest event in Christian history — the resurrection of Christ, who was the unconquerable Sun.

In the house-churches of the apostolic age the worshipers seem either to have stood, with arms and heads raised for prayer, or to have prostrated themselves. Only with the passing centuries did they generally kneel or cross their arms by placing hands on opposite shoulders. The folding of hands in prayer was taken over even later from the custom of a feudal fief's placing his hands in the hands of his lord, a gesture of trust and commitment. The lowering of the head and the closing of eyes for prayer seem to come from the penitential and introspective tendencies of Pietism.

The officiant faced out across the holy table, in what has become known as the westward position, when he celebrated the Eucharist, and at some points in the ceremony he was seated. One or two of the earliest house-churches give at least some indication that both priest and people at various times faced east, with the altar in the west, though to our senses it does not seem very liturgical to have the priest looking at the backs of his people or the people looking away from the altar. Consecrating the elements of the Eucharist across the altar, in full sight of the people, appears to have been the normal pattern until the 11th or 12th century. At that time the mushrooming growth of painted altarpieces blocked off the back of the altar and forced the priest to stand *between* altar and people and consecrate with his back turned to the congregation.

Though there seems to have been no standard place from which to read the Scriptures, except from the altar itself, a reading desk, or ambo, made an appearance and, in the large late-medieval churches, with their acoustic problems, developed gradually into what we now know as lectern. This usually stood at the dividing point of chancel and nave, or choir and nave, with the pulpit sometimes within the nave.

The rapid growth of the church, along with the burgeoning of the monastic movement, gave great impetus to the multiplication of services and times of services. By the 11th or the 12th century, the monks had almost single-handedly turned the once-weekly or thrice-weekly mass into a daily one, or a twice- or thrice-daily one. For the first four or five centuries of the Christian era the Eucharist appears to have been largely restricted to Sunday and the major festivals, with occasional celebrations in larger centers also on the station days of Wednesday and Friday.

The monks at an early date adapted the traditional hours of prayer of the Jews. For the Hebrews these had numbered seven, as the psalmist stated (119:164): "Seven times a day do I praise Thee, because of Thy righteous judgments." In practice the Jews usually stopped at three, with these falling at the third, sixth, and ninth hours. Daniel was thrown to the lions because he insisted on praying thrice daily. (Dan. 6:10)

The Christians also seem to have kept the Hebraic times of private worship and to have prayed at regular hours. In the monasteries these developed into full and complete services, or "offices": Matins, Lauds, Prime, Terce, Sext, None, Vespers, and Compline, corresponding to the psalmist's "seven times a day," if the first two are considered one continuous service. Generally these canonical offices fell every three hours, from three in the morning until late at night. In the monastery chapels they were observed with a prescribed liturgy composed mainly of the common recital of Psalms; in the homes of the rich and the the quarters of the priests they were usually marked by private readings or devotions.

For priests the appropriate readings were called breviaries; for laymen, books of hours. In the cottages of the peasants, or out in the fields, the canonical offices were usually observed with the sign of the cross and a pious prayer as the church bells tolled out the hour. The best known of these observances is the Angelus ("The angel of the Lord declared unto Mary . . ."), said three times a day to recall the Lord's incarnation.

In the Lutheran and Anglican churches the offices of Matins (spelled Mattins in the Book of Common Prayer) and of Vespers are still in common use, just as they were throughout the Middle Ages. Nowadays they usually combine certain elements from the offices of other canonical hours as well. Luther urged that Matins and Vespers be held in parish churches on both Sundays and festivals, since this form of service contained almost nothing but Scriptures and was an excellent method of proclaiming the Word. Generally the major parts of these offices include: Hymnody, Psalmody, Lessons, and Prayers.

For a Christian of the 20th century to conceive of church life as it might have been in the 10th or even in the 15th century is nearly impossible. A good deal of romanticizing has gone on—but some of it quite justified. Great cathedrals like those of Chartres or Canterbury or Santiago de Campostela still witness majestically to the faith and dedication of their era.

On the other hand one must also recall the constant use of charms to ward off the devil, a general ignorance of the Scriptures, a lack of interest in preaching even by the clergy, and the use of a language which none but the educated could understand. When Pope Zacharias (d. 752), for example, wrote to Boniface, the apostle of Germany, he complained of priests who knew so little Latin that they mistakenly baptized not in the name of the Father (*patris*) but of the fatherland (*patriae*), and not in the name of the Son (*filii*) but of the daughter (*filiae*).

What was even worse, the use of a tongue unknown to the people made the mass appear to be a kind of magical act they were not expected to understand and could not participate in. We get our word "hocus-pocus" from a corruption of the Latin *hoc est corpus meum* ("this is My body"). Unfortunately the clergy became involved in developing new "uses" and forms, each more elaborate than its predecessor. Worst of all was the mushrooming of the votive masses, said in exchange for a fee and without a congregation, usually for the souls of the dead. In some areas a third of all the men in the community were priests or monks.

On the other hand the church's interest in liturgy and worship was a sign of health. Some theologians argue that this great proliferation tended to obscure the central message of Christ become man. Yet in an age when communication was poor and learning was rare, the church had to serve both as entertainer and teacher, first winning the attention of serf or craftsman and then involving him in an act of faith. Some of the church's devices toward this end (broadly speaking, "sacramentals") were candles, incense, rosaries, and pilgrimages.

At the time of the apostles the normal lights at the altar, just as in the home, were lamps of olive oil. These were long a tradition of Christian worship, especially in the dark catacombs and basilicas of the Byzantine age. They were a practical necessity but also tended to symbolize Christ as the Light, the Sun, the Morning Star.

When candles became cheaper, they gradually replaced the oil lamps, especially in areas where there were no olive groves. Selling candles to the faithful, who brought them into the nave and lighted them before an altar, usually as a votive light, that is, as a request *(votum,* "wish") that a specific boon be granted, was a mixed blessing.

Though the practice brought in considerable money—in some places and at some times it was the church's chief source of income—to some it recalled the objections Jesus had raised about those who had turned His Father's house into a den of thieves. Most worshipers, however, probably were well aware that they were actually supporting the church as they paid their coins and were not trying to buy favors with God.

Originally candles were made almost exclusively of beeswax. Unfortunately this is considerably stickier than that made from animal or vegetable oils, and it melts in hot weather. Now many non-Roman churches use candles of stearine, made from petroleum, or tallow, from animal fats, though for the sake of tradition others insist that the candle must be at least 51 percent beeswax.

Christians generally agree that candles are a touching and meaningful symbol of the light God has given in Christ to a darkened world. Although today we have much more powerful lights available, the quiet glow of the traditional candle seems more meditative and festive than electric lights. Tradition varies as to how many candles should be used. There is the saying by Innocent III from the time of the Crusades: "Two lighted candles are placed at the ends of the altar to signify the joy of the Jews and the Gentiles at the birth of Christ."

Incense was at first so closely connected with the pagan mystery cults of Greece and Egypt so popular in the Roman Empire that Christians did not light it, despite its use in the Jewish temple. Burning a cone of incense was also a standard method of swearing allegiance to the Roman emperor and of paying him divine honors. Naturally this ceased when Constantine adopted the Christian faith and set aside emperor worship.

At what time incense became a part of Christian worship is not very certain. Apparently it was used in the East earlier than in the West, perhaps first as a fumigant (for instance, in funeral processions) and then ritually. Constantine himself presented a golden censor to the bishop of Rome, and since Constantine loved the splendor and pageantry of Constantinople, no one quite knows whether the gift was intended for the church or the palace. In the Byzantine churches, influenced by the ceremonial of the imperial court, incense came to be used especially as a way to honor Christ as He was symbolically making His entry among the worshipers in the procession bringing forward the gospel.

By the sixth century there is an occasional mention of incense in the West, though there are generally no rubrics about it in any family of uses until the Romano-Frankish ones of the time of Charlemagne and Alcuin. As late as the 13th century incense must still have been somewhat unusual in the West, since St. Thomas Aquinas writes that its primary purpose is to cleanse the church of must and mold. Only in a secondary sense was it a "sweet-smelling savor unto the Lord," symbolizing the prayers of the faithful ascending to the throne of God. "Let my prayer be set forth before Thee as incense," the Psalmist prayed.

Pilgrimages were a lively and useful element of earlier Christianity, especially those to the burial place of a martyr. Despite the problems that pilgrimages often presented, as one can see even from the most superficial reading of Chaucer's *Canterbury Tales,* for the most part they were a credit to the church. What Luther was critical of was their being interpreted as something meritorious before God, as if God's grace were not free and could not be found at home.

Yet the believer who could honestly wear the sign to show that he had journeyed to Jerusalem (the crossed palms), or to Rome (the keys of St. Peter), or to the shrine of St. James at Santiago de Campostela (the scallop shell), had probably deepened his spiritual understanding through his pilgrimage. Pilgrimages — travel on foot to faraway, hallowed places, widened the horizons of men, provided for travel with a goal and meaning, and stimulated meditation and devotion.

Even in little things the church showed itself a responsible teacher and guardian. In an age when the lamp of learning flickered but dimly, the church made excellent use of miracle plays and mystery plays, at first in the chancel and then on the church steps, or in the marketplace, to help teach the stories of the Bible. The Passion Play at Oberammergau or the Passion Weeks in Spain are relics of this concern.

With the help of stained-glass pictorialization, as in the cathedral at Chartres, the faithful could meditate on the events of the gospel, even though almost none of them could read or could even have afforded a Bible before the age of printing. The leper's squint, a clear window near the chancel, where those with a communicable disease could nonetheless view the Sacrament or watch the celebration from the outside, was a further touch of thoughtfulness and consideration.

So was the practice of inscribing in a special logbook the names of those who supplied the wine and bread or the custom of ceremoniously disposing of the water used in baptism through the special drain known as the piscina.

Excesses there may have been in ritual and custom, but so far as it was able the church became all things to all men that it might bring all to the knowledge of Christ.

4

Advent — God's Coming

THE BEGINNING OF THE CHURCH YEAR

For the first two or three centuries the church year began not with Christmas or Advent but with Easter. Not only were the death and the resurrection the most important events in the life of Christ; mid-March was also the beginning of the Roman year. The mood of the new year is still echoed in the Epistle and Gospel for Septuagesima, as well as by the Old Testament lessons for Matins and Vespers, which tell of God's creation of the world.

By the fourth century, however, perhaps because of the southward push of the Germanic tribes, who began their new year in midwinter, the beginning of the church year in the West had moved back to Christmas or Epiphany. Epiphany was still somewhat more important than Christmas — one of the times when new catechumens were received into the church, even as the Wise Men had come to find their Savior. In the East the church year still begins with Easter.

The beginning of the church year moved back from the Christmas-Epiphany period to the beginning of Advent about the eighth century. This season was at first a time of fasting and meditation for those who were preparing for baptism, chiefly on Epiphany. Such preparation was common in the churches of the East but not so common in Rome. Advent seems to have entered the Western calendar through Spain and France.

In any event, the three or four weeks of a penitential mood which immediately preceded Christmas were already becoming known as Advent, the Latin word for "Coming." Often this began as early as St. Martin's Day, November 11.

The mood of Advent, unlike that of Lent, was in Rome not one of sorrow but of holy joy. Several of the Latin fathers suggest that Advent developed as an antidote to the midwinter festivals of the ancient Germans, with their lavish excesses of food and drink.

In the Latin church today, Advent is among the *tempora clausa,* the closed periods when church members are urged to postpone such joyous festivities as weddings and parties. Originally the proper color for Advent was white, signifying joy and celebration and festivity, as was proper for the coming of Christ.

When Johann Sebastian Bach was director of music at St. Thomas School in Leipzig in the 1700s, the choir boys traditionally sang no motets or chorales during Advent, nor was there any congregational singing. Despite the ban during the services, however, Advent was a popular time for concerts and recitals. In the Roman rite the practice often was to omit the Te Deum and the Gloria in Excelsis but to retain the Hallelujahs.

Nowadays Advent begins with the Sunday nearest St. Andrew's Day, November 30. This means that there are always four Sundays in Advent. The first is known as Advent Sunday, considered somewhat more significant than the others. The theme of the first Sunday was Christ's entry into Jerusalem, and that of the second was His coming as judge—Christ the Pantocrator. The third Sunday, Gaudete, was more joyous in mood, introducing John the Baptist as Christ's forerunner, and the fourth presented John's testimony to Christ.

The collects for the Sundays in Advent always began with the words "Stir up," and are jokingly called the *stirrup* prayers. The collect for the last Sunday after Trinity also began in the same fashion, a trace of those ancient calendars when Advent began a Sunday or two earlier than it does now.

The split personality of the Advent season—holy fear and holy joy—is reflected in its Lessons. Advent depicts the long-awaited coming of Christ as the just judge of the world, as the fulfillment of ancient prophecies, and at the same time as a peaceful Messiah on a humble donkey. In John the Baptist we see a recluse who eats honey and locusts in the desert but also an evangelist who shouts: "Prepare ye the way of the Lord!"

The mood of Advent seems to have varied from area to area. In Scandinavia it appears to have been far more joyous than around the Mediterranean. Perhaps this was the influence of the midwinter Nordic revels. During the fourth century one of the popes was so perturbed by extremes of costume and of drinking he even considered doing away with Christmas. What he objected to specifically was that newly converted Christians appeared hopelessly drunk on the streets and even came to church intoxicated and in the skins of wild animals.

By the time of the Middle Ages a whole series of customs, some Christian, some pagan, had grown up around Advent. The celebrations in honor of Saint Barbara, Saint Lucy, and Saint Nicholas were gradually related to the birth of Christ.

St. Lucy

St. Lucy, whose day falls on December 13, was originally a girl of Sicily who was martyred by Diocletian and finally buried in Venice. The famous folksong *Santa Lucia* reminds us that she was the patron of the gondoliers. Her name really means "light," and nowhere was she so much honored as in those countries of the north where the wintry nights were the darkest and the longest.

Before the calendar reform, the feast day honoring Lucy fell on the shortest day of the year. This was the same day when the Germanic countries celebrated the turn of the seasons—the greatest of their annual feasts. This circumstance made Lucy one of the most honored of the saints.

Wherever Scandinavians have settled, December 13th is still a major day of rejoicing. In each family a "Lucy bride" takes the part of the saint, and in each community the most attractive "Lucy bride" represents them all. Ordinarily she wears a wreath of greenery and candles in her hair, and besides reigning over the happy day, goes around waking up her family with coffee and cakes. The pastry she makes is called *lussekattor* or Lucy cats—rich fat muffins, perhaps as much a sign of good luck as cats once were.

On the Continent the massive bonfires built at the time of the winter solstice seem to have had much in common with those of the vernal equinox, as best known in the rites of the Druids. Both of course centered on the worship of the sun.

The church made Lucy the patron of light and fire. The collects of the Christmas season reveal some of this old fear of darkness when they proclaim that Christ is the light of the world. Lucy appears to be a minor light, something like a female John the Baptist, to help prepare the way for the Christ. After the calendar reforms St. Lucy's Day fell a dozen days earlier.

St. Nicholas

The story of St. Nicholas and how he came to be the modern Santa Claus is almost as complicated as the story of St. Lucy. As a minor bishop in Asia Minor, Nicholas had never really seemed very memorable, despite the legends of his kindness and popularity. Yet around the shores of the Aegean he was very popular; when the church needed a good man to embellish the Christmas story, Nicholas was a natural.

Of the many stories and miracles that are told of him the most widespread was probably that of the three maidens. Daughters of a rich merchant who had lost his wealth, they were now destined to become old maids because their father could no longer afford dowries.

St. Nicholas provided bags of gold sovereigns for all three, who were then happily married. And from that story—Nicholas with bags of gold over his shoulder—comes the modern version of a Santa Claus with a bag of toys.

The activities of St. Nicholas Day often included a major service, with the sermon delivered by a boy bishop, a procession, a huge feast, and the gathering of alms among the nobles and townspeople. Collecting these alms for St. Nicholas has given us another symbol—the three balls of the pawnbroker.

These three balls also represent the three bags of gold Nicholas once gave to the merchant's daughters, which Nicholas acquired by begging and borrowing. Somehow Nicholas came to be the patron saint of the pawnbrokers, and the medieval symbol of three golden balls is still a sign of the trade today.

That St. Nicholas came to be one of the most popular saints in Holland, Switzerland, and Russia is not really very significant, except that the American version of Santa Claus seems to have come from Holland. The Dutch settlers brought him along to New Amsterdam and taught their children to hang stockings over the hearth. Apparently the stockings represented St. Nicholas' bags of gold, but now they were filled with candy, nuts, and fruit.

The importance of New York as a center of trade and the chance popularity of a famous poem of Dr. Clement Moore soon made Saint Nicholas—or rather Santa Claus—famous. Outside New York not one child in twenty had ever heard of Santa Claus, not before the famous "'Twas the Night Before Christmas." In one generation Santa Claus became a kind of American patron saint.

The Spirit of Advent

The spirit of Advent is not merely one of joyous feasting or gift-giving, as the customs suggested by Lucy and Nicholas might indicate. The proper spirit is best summed up in the words of the ancient plain-song dating from the time of the Crusades:

> Oh, come, Oh, come, Emmanuel,
> And ransom captive Israel
> That mourns in lonely exile here
> Until the Son of God appear.
> Rejoice! Rejoice! Emmanuel
> Shall come to thee, O Israel.

This hymn breathes the spirit of the ancient churches of Gaul and Spain, where the annual coming of Christ was awaited with special joy and reverence. In fact, it was these churches that introduced the whole season of Advent and perhaps even of Christmas.

With the coming of December 16th a new note of urgency invades the Advent liturgy. "The Golden Nights" of Advent begin then, lasting until Christmas Eve, when a series of antiphons known as the "O's of Advent" reflect the church's excitement and eagerness.

The "O's of Advent" are responsive chants based on passages of Scripture. Those from the Old Testament foretell the Messiahship of Christ, and those from the New testify to His Sonship. In these joyous responses Christ is variously addressed as: "O Wisdom," "O Lord of Lords," "O Root of Jesse," "O Key of David," "O Dawning Brightness," "O King and Desire of Nations," and "O Emmanuel." In the whole field of liturgy the antiphons of the Advent season are a classic example of the best in Christian worship—words well mated to meaningful and relevant ideas.

Another popular part of the Advent liturgy in some Christian churches is the Te Deum. This famous chant strongly emphasizes both the first and the second coming of Christ. His birth is summarized in the words: "When Thou tookest upon Thee to deliver man, Thou didst humble Thyself to be born of a virgin." His second coming is specifically mentioned in the words: "We believe that Thou shalt come to be our Judge."

In many areas the fortnight before Christmas was one long holiday, often known as the "Golden Nights." In northern Europe these weeks were marked by a custom known as "Searching for an Inn."

The searching was done by a group from the church, representing Mary and Joseph and moving from house to house, asking whether there was room to be taken in. This was a very meaningful rite, since it reminded the whole community of their need to open their hearths and homes to the Christ Child. Martin Luther may well have had this custom in mind as he wrote in the Christmas hymn "From Heaven Above to Earth I Come":

> Ah, dearest Jesus, holy Child
> Make Thee a bed, soft, undefiled,
> Within my heart that it may be
> A quiet chamber kept for Thee.

Southern Europe had a similar custom known as the Inn, or the *Posada*. Here the householders set up in their own homes a cradle or manger for the Christ Child. Since the cradle remained empty, it differed significantly from the later custom of making a crèche, or *presepio,* a three-dimensional layout depicting all the sacred characters of the Christmas story—the angels, shepherds, Wise Men, Mary, Joseph, Jesus, Herod, and the Holy Innocents.

At the time of Luther a real cradle often became the focus of family devotions. Many an ancient Christmas carol was sung around the cradle, and the rhythms were distinctly those of lullabies. Over the centuries, however, a good many superstitions began to creep in, and church authorities discouraged such singing round the cradle.

Probably the commonest of family customs is the Advent wreath. Though the story of holiday greenery really belongs to Christmas, the wreath at least belongs to Advent. This custom seems to have grown up among the old Germanic clans, but now it is a living tradition in thousands of homes and churches.

The Advent wreath, made of laurel, pine, holly, bayberry, or any evergreen, symbolizes the eternity of God and of the human soul. At one time it may have represented a Teutonic fire wheel, a symbol of the sun gods, but to Christians the perfect circle and the green of the evergreens meant eternity.

The number of candles and how they were lighted varied considerably, even in those areas around the Baltic where the Advent wreath seems to have originated. The commonest form was a wreath with four candles, one for each of the Sundays in Advent.

In some churches larger candles represented the Sundays and smaller ones the week days. Others added some other symbol to mark off the week days—a cluster of berries or a pine cone, for example.

Often the Advent wreath became a center of family devotions, an intriguing way to interest children in the coming of the Savior. Unfortunately the modern world has crowded out many of these pleasant old Christian customs, but this one is certainly worth reviving in any Christian home.

5

The Feast of the Nativity

THE MEANING OF CHRISTMAS

If Mary and Joseph were to see a modern Christmas, they might very well wonder what the festival was about. The story of the Infant in the manger, of the Wise Men and the shepherds, is so tinseled over with feasting and giving, with wassailing and commercializing, that one has to dig deep to find the real meaning.

Yet getting ready for the newborn King does not mean that children have to go without their plates of cookies, mailmen without their trucks of greetings, or supermarkets without their bundles of balsams. If the child of God really understands the reason for his celebrating, there is nothing wrong with celebrating. But if he celebrates just to be celebrating, without knowing why, then Christmas is no longer Christmas.

This is the problem that generation after generation of God's people have faced. In Puritan England the followers of Cromwell were so convinced Christmas had become completely paganized they turned it into a normal work day.

Very early in the life of the church there was considerable discussion whether Christ's birth, as opposed to His death and resurrection, should be celebrated at all. Origen (185?–254?), one of the earliest and most respected of theologians, argued that Christ was not a Pharaoh and that to remember His day of birth might well class Him as an earthly prince, not as God.

Apparently other churchmen agreed, because in the chief centers of the church—Jerusalem, Antioch, Constantinople, Alexandria, Ephesus—the birthday of Christ was not a part of the Christian calendar until centuries after Easter and Pentecost were well established. By the early 300s, however, Christmas began to be celebrated rather regularly.

It commemorated not only Christ's birth (technically, The Nativity) but also His baptism and His second coming—the latter a theme that dominated the whole of the church's thinking. As in the case of other early Christian celebrations, the celebration was not a historical anniversary of a certain event but a celebration of God's gifts to us in Christ.

The Date of Christmas

The change in date from January 6th to December 25th seems to have been influenced mostly by the midwinter celebrations of the pagans. The holidays of the Germanic tribes fell near the end of December, and in the calendar of that period the winter solstice was the 25th. The Romans celebrated it as the Nativity of the Unconquerable Sun.

The Christians borrowed the symbolism of the winter solstice. Christ was called the Sun of righteousness, He whose star had risen in the East and who would appear again from the East at His second coming. Ancient prayers for the Christmas season reflect this imagery as they describe how the Father "made this most holy night shine with the brightness of the true Light."

Unlike the modern celebration of Christmas, the ancient one was considered not so much a day as a season. The spirit of Christmas really began with Advent, at the end of November, and continued right up until Candlemas, February 2d, when Christ was presented at the temple. Liturgically, the Christmas cycle lasts until the pre-Easter season, until Septuagesima.

In a stricter sense Christmas began on December 25th and ended on January 6th, with Epiphany, known in England as Twelfth Night (after Christmas). The special emphasis which the church continued to place on Epiphany, together with the practice (still alive in Spain, Portugal, and France) of exchanging gifts not on Christmas but on the day of the Wise Men, turned Christmas into one long fortnight.

Even as recently as the era of our grandparents Christmas services were held not only on Christmas Eve and Christmas Day but also on Second Christmas Day and on Third Christmas Day. Second Christmas Day also marked the martyrdom of Stephen, stoned in Jerusalem, and Third Christmas Day also honored the apostle John, exiled on the island of Patmos.

As at Easter, the church of the Middle Ages stressed three services on Christmas Day: at midnight, at dawn, and at the normal midmorning hour. In Sweden, where the state church is Lutheran, tradition strongly accents the dawn service. There it is thought that the shepherds first heard the angels at midnight and first found the Child at dawn.

Christmas Customs

What makes the American Christmas interesting is its wide range of customs. This was once true also at Rome, when envoys and merchants from all over the empire streamed home for the holidays. But even then the bishops complained about the many pagan customs being brought in from the far corners of the world.

The majority of Christmas customs are of pagan origin. The more picturesque include decorating with evergreens and candles, singing carols, preparing food and drink, sending Christmas cards, visiting friends, giving presents, helping the poor, and bringing in the Yule log.

One of the oldest of these is the use of greens—fir, pine, palm, laurel, rosemary, holly, ivy, fern, mistletoe. Though such plants and flowers have an ancient tradition even in Christianity, many of the specific practices seem to come from the folk religion of the Teutonic tribes.

Even in the Eastern Church, which was little affected by the nomadic invasions from the North, the use of palms, olive leaves, and flowers was common. This living greenery served exactly as it had when Christ told of the lilies of the field, the unfruitful fig tree, the stalks of wheat, and the fruitful vine.

For a time the church seems to have opposed the use of greens. Even as late as the eighth century, Boniface, the apostle of Northern Europe, felt he needed the specific approval of the pope before he could perpetuate their use in Christian services.

Though in one dramatic incident this saint chopped down an oak sacred to the god Thor, more often he let the forest people retain their shrines. Meanwhile he tried to explain that the God they really sought was not Woden or Thor but Christ. When he received classes of catechumens on Palm Sunday or Pentecost, he had them wear fruit blossoms and carry fresh fronds of birch and beech, which in earlier times had been a rite of their springtime festivals. He also encouraged them to continue tying a fir tree to the rafters of a house they were building, to bring good luck to the owners and protect the workmen from accident.

The use of mistletoe is perhaps the clearest example of a non-Christian custom that has become Christianized. Mistletoe is a parasite and seeks its nourishment not from the earth but from another plant. As a part of their winter sun-worship the Druid priests solemnly gathered mistletoe, using golden sickles which they had specially consecrated.

The yellow-green leaves and the waxen-white berries were not allowed to touch the ground. Gathered in the ceremonial cloak of the Druid, they were distributed to the faithful, one sprig to each family, and the rest was burned on a special altar as an appeasement of the gods.

In the Dark Ages mistletoe was considered one of the most potent drugs and charms. Monks called it "the wood of the sacred cross," apparently to ward off evil spells. By and large it was classified in the same category as black cats, goblins, and leprechauns. Even today many think that mistletoe should not hang in church because of its pagan associations.

The story of the Christmas tree is buried just as deeply in the history of our pagan forefathers as that of mistletoe. Evergreens of one sort or another have been a part of Christmas for centuries, and some scholars say one can find them even in the hieroglyphs of Egypt and the scrolls of Babylon.

Several of the later Roman poets wrote of a tree that was brought indoors in the winter and decorated with tufts of paper and masks of Bacchus, the god of wine and revelry. The German tribes thought that bringing a tree into their homes was a little like bringing in God. In fact, they placed offerings on the branches—apples, cakes, and candies. Occasionally the tree was even dedicated to the sun god.

The popularity of the Christmas tree today is often ascribed to Martin Luther. Most likely it was during his lifetime that the lighted and decorated tree once again became popular after a long period of neglect.

Be that as it may, Christmas trees began to be common in Germany in the 17th and 18th centuries and spread to Scandinavia and England in the 19th. Even today they are alien to Romance countries like Spain and Portugal.

The earliest American tree we know of was one in the 1820s at the home of a German professor at Harvard. Writing a decade later, his wife mentions that her husband had set up a tree for their son and that it had caused considerable comment.

Apparently no one dared bring a tree into church for another 20 years. Pastors preached sermons to the effect that children should celebrate Christmas reading the Bible rather than dancing around a tree.

The first Christmas tree we know of in a church was one put up in Cleveland in 1851 by a Lutheran pastor named Schwan. He nearly split the parish. Half his elders objected violently, considering the tree pagan. Scholar that he was, the good pastor dug up some ancient references to show that the use of evergreens was an old and established custom, and by the following Christmas he not only had a tree in church but also one in the home of the elder who had most strongly opposed him.

The most significant development in the Christmas tree has probably been the switch from candles to electric lights. This was largely for reasons of safety. Yet the pleasant scent of burning candles was a memory many youngsters now miss. They also miss the joy of decorating a tree with the efforts of their own hands. Trimming a tree with nuts, fruit, foil, sugar cubes, candy, cranberries, and popcorn was one of the greatest delights of our grandparents.

Part of this joy a wise parent can still recover. Nothing helps a child understand quite so much what Christmas is all about as making his own decorations. With metaled string, with a stack of old Christmas cards, with construction paper, the only limit is the child's imagination.

Some children like to concentrate on the various symbols that represent Christ, such as the IHC of the Greek name for Jesus. For others, especially if they are small, a simple picture of the Wise Men or the shepherds, cut from last year's cards and pasted on two sides of a piece of bright paper, is both attractive and original — far better than a bit of blown glass and tinsel.

Symbols from the Old Testament also make an unusual tree — perhaps a "tree of Jesse." These might include paper apples recalling the story of Adam and Eve, or the two tables of the Law, the flaming lanterns of Gideon, the star of David, or the dove that flew from the ark — anything, in fact, that recalls how the people of Israel awaited their Savior. Such a project is an ideal occasion for a mother to tell her children the stories of the Old Testament.

Besides the Christmas tree and the mistletoe, another common decoration is holly. One legend suggests that it was a holly bush which Moses saw as the burning bush, but this is quite unlikely. The list of Christmas plants — cactus, poinsettia, Jerusalem cherry, cyclamen — is almost endless. One popular older theme was that the whole plant world sprang to life to honor Christ's birth.

The Yule log was traditional especially among the English, even though it got its start in Scandinavia. The goddess of the hearth was always a popular one in the North, and the ceremonial lighting of the Yule log was sometimes believed to reflect Christ's status as the Light of the world. At least this was how some of the pious revelers explained the custom to their priests. The drinking, storytelling, feasting, and procession that often went with the lighting of the Yule log were a general part of the month-long festival of midwinter.

Ever since Christmas first began to be celebrated, there was strong dissension between those who wanted to remember it as a day of prayer and meditation and those who felt it was a time of holiday-making and feasting. One custom which accented both was that of the *presepio,* or crèche.

St. Francis was its greatest popularizer, even though there had once been crèches in Rome six centuries earlier. To try to bring the Bible to life, Francis sought the pope's permission to set up a "living" stable, complete with animals and people, to act out the parts of those who made their way to Bethlehem that sacred night.

As St. Bonaventure recounted the story a generation later, the townsfolk were so impressed by this outdoor manger that they demanded a repeat performance year after year, complete with lanterns, shepherds, angels, and carols.

The idea of depicting the events of Christ's birth with images of cork, pottery, china, and wood grew equally popular. Even the hut of the simplest peasant often boasted such a manger scene.

The most famous manger scene is probably that in the Church of Cosmas and Damian in Rome. It measures three stories high and is the size of a tennis court. What makes this *presepio* famous is the quality of the wood carving, the jewels that adorn the Wise Men, and the artistic insight that has put so much into so little space. It boasts whole villages and castles, orchards with fruit trees, fields of grain, maids baking bread, and servants scrubbing the floor.

In Spain and Portugal the life-size *presepios* often included far more than just the central story of Christ's birth. One can often find dozens of other tableaux depicting such incidents as the appearance of the Wise Men before Herod, the annunciation of Jesus to Joseph, the visit of Mary to her cousin Elisabeth, and the slaughter of the Holy Innocents, all done in a sometimes too bloody and realistic Iberian fashion.

At first glance Christmas carols would seem to be solely religious, though at one time many of the carols were not considered proper for use in church. A few modern hymnals still list carols separately from hymns, as if the carol more properly belonged in the home or the street.

The origin of the word carol helps to explain the problem—a problem that led the Puritans to ban all singing at Christmas. The word carol really means a dance, a dance in which ancient pagan revelers joined hands and circled round a fire, singing as they went.

Basically, a carol is a folksong, changed and improved as it passed from generation to generation, simpler and more lyrical than a hymn, and often with less theology. Samples of older carols would include: "I Saw Three Ships Come Sailing," "The First Noel," "The Cherry Tree Carol," "The Holly and the Ivy," and "God Rest You Merry, Gentlemen."

In modern times the story of a seminary professor's Christmas poem that embarrassed him because it had so little religion is a parallel to the origin of many ancient carols. This is the story of Clement Clarke Moore's "'Twas the Night Before Christmas."

Moore, a professor at the General Theological Seminary in New York, wrote the poem in 1822 to amuse his children. Little did he know that he was establishing the bewhiskered and rolypoly figure of the Dutch Santa Claus as the patron saint of Christmas.

The poem probably would never have seen print had it not been for a friend who visited him, heard it, and thought it so delightful that she begged permission to copy it. The next year she sent it to a newspaper, and within a few years it was being reprinted across the country.

This was quite an embarrassment to the professor, who didn't really consider it the kind of thing a Christian and a gentleman ought to write, especially one who taught theology. Not until more than 20 years later did he confess that it was his.

The notion of Christmas as a time of plays, pantomimes, feasting, and reveling is largely English in origin. Probably at one time the custom extended right across northern Europe, where the English once came from, but it was they who developed it most.

The whole notion of an Anglo-Saxon Christmas seemed to be one of merrymaking and gourmandizing. Even as early as the days of King Alfred, at the end of the ninth century, the twelve days of Christmas were formally proclaimed by royal decree. At one of these brawls the Anglo-Saxons were so addleheaded from their mead they were completely surrounded by a band of Danish invaders. According to legend, King Alfred pretended to be the court fool and delighted his conquerors so much they gave him his freedom, without ever discovering who he really was.

A "Lord of Misrule," somewhat like a modern master of ceremonies, presided over the festivities with the aid of the court jester. It was he who arranged for plays and pantomimes, for singing, for dancing, for music, and for the various games and entertainments.

Many of the games were those that are still reasonably well known, such as bobbing for apples. Others were of a more sporting variety. In snapdragon, the players tried to snatch raisins from a bowl of burning spirits. Many a burnt finger and many a challenge made this game a favorite not only of the young swains who played but also of the maidens who egged them on.

During the daytime, hunting and falconing ate up a good chunk of the holidays. Wagering made the sport even more exciting. When the hunt was for game as large as deer or boar, the ladies of the court usually had to be escorted at a safe distance by pages. Tournaments, archery, dancing, and various kinds of skits and plays, either of a religious or a comical theme, were also a standard part of Christmas.

If there was one factor that dominated the holidays, it was eating and drinking. The Germanic tribes had always had a reputation for drinking, and the ale and mead flowed even more plentifully in Merrie Olde England. We get our word *wassail* from them. Wassail really means nothing more than the modern toast, "Your health!" In Anglo-Saxon the words were *waes hael* — "may you be healthy." Caroling and wassailing were often inseparable as a group of fun-makers went about the countryside singing.

To many an Englishman Christmas suggested eating. At one Christmas feast, in the 13th century, the archbishop of York provided his guests with 600 steers. King Richard II (1367—1400) once hired 2,000 cooks to prepare a Christmas feast and served 20,000 guests.

Meat dishes included a dozen kinds of fish, oysters, beef, venison, pork, boar, hare, swan, turkey, heron, duck, goose, capon, and peacock. Traditionally the most important were the wild boar and the peacock. The boar was often served whole, his jaws stuffed with an apple, his skin soaked with brandy and set afire.

Wild boars were still reasonably common in the forests, and they were hunted with great pleasure. After the Battle of Hastings in 1066, English meats assumed French names. Boar became "brawn," cow became "beef," deer became "venison," and pig became "pork." As the boar was ceremoniously trundled into the great hall, where he would be carved by the master of the feast, the crowd joined in the singing of the Boar's Head Carol.

The peacock was almost as famous a meat for lords and ladies as was brawn. The skin and feathers were carefully removed, the bird roasted, and then the skin put back in place. With its head erect and its plumage glistening, often with a gilded beak and flaming spirits, the peacock was borne proudly into the hall. The honor of carrying the platter, or at least leading the procession, went to the lady of the house, followed by a band of minstrels performing on the flutes and zithers.

The peacock was an especial favorite of the sporting crowd, a common dish at the time of tournaments. Often the knights swore to perform their vows by raising their swords over the peacock, and the ladies in turn swore their faithfulness.

With the supply of food and drink so plentiful, the behavior during the days of Christmas often got out of hand. The Puritans openly preached against wild merrymaking, arguing that it was a disservice to Christ. With the Civil War in 1642 came further drastic reforms. Celebrating Christmas in any form, even if it were with a service in church, a Bible reading at home, or the singing of hymns round the hearth, was considered heathen and banned.

Parliament passed laws banning Christmas, Easter, and Pentecost — the three major festivals of the church year. Christmas Day was to be a workday; shops were to remain open; Parliament was to sit; services of any kind were forbidden. No one could light any more candles than he lit on any other night, and the food he ate was supposed to be the same as on any other day.

Naturally those who were not sympathetic to Cromwell could not really be forced to comply, even though in a few towns the criers went through the streets shouting, "No Christmas today, no Christmas today!" In England a few clergymen were actually jailed for conducting services, together with a sprinkling of layfolk who had the courage to join them. Others simply bolted the doors behind them and went on with Christmas as usual.

What makes the Puritan period especially interesting is its influence on America. For the first 10 or 20 years the Puritans of Massachusetts were so much in the majority that they were able to influence the whole pattern of the American Christmas.

For 40 years these new Americans, including some who were not of the Puritan persuasion, worked on Christmas Day. The only exemption was for those who wished to stay at home and meditate, though on one occasion Governor Bradford disciplined certain men who confused meditating with playing ball. The singing of carols and hymns was also banned.

Though a mass of new settlers continually weakened the Puritan stranglehold, especially when these newcomers began to include Anglicans, Reformed, Lutherans, and Roman Catholics, Christmas did not become a legal holiday in Massachusetts until a few years before the Civil War.

But to tell the truth, the Puritans were not wholly wrong. A Christmas without Christ was no Christmas at all. The birth of the Savior had in some times and some places been an excuse not to thank and worship Him but to feed one's belly and get drunk. The Puritans' mistake was that in casting out the excesses of Christmas they had also cast out the Christ Child.

6

The Twelve Days of Christmas

Ask a child when Christmas ends, and the likely answer is "Never." In terms of the Christian year, that's not bad. The spirit of Christmas runs through the Scripture readings and prayers from Advent until Lent. Originally the entire two weeks between December 25th and January 6th were the celebration of Christ's "Coming," with Epiphany as a part of the Christmas cycle. In fact, the former name for Epiphany was "Old Christmas."

Nowadays festivals like those of St. Stephen and St. John seem almost to intrude on the spirit of Christmas, though by ancient tradition these are a very part of Christmas. Just as a Greek iconostasis or a Ravenna mosaic surrounds Christ with His most intimate friends and associates, so also did the ancient church cluster saints' days about the day of Christ's Nativity — the days of John, Stephen, Peter, Paul, Mary, Joseph, and James, "the brother of the Lord."

ST. STEPHEN

Until recently December 26 was an important day of obligation, that is, a day when all good Christians were expected to attend service. It was important not only because it continued the theme of Christmas but also because it was the day of St. Stephen.

The Book of Acts tells how Stephen, whose name in Greek means "crowned," was stoned to death in Jerusalem and became the first of the Christian martyrs. In the medieval world Stephen was extremely popular. Great cathedrals like the ones in Vienna and Budapest were built to his memory. The carol "Good King Wenceslas" tells what happened on St. Stephen's Day in 10th-century Bohemia.

Perhaps because the farm animals rested during the Christmas holidays or perhaps because they were present in the stable when Christ was born, Stephen came to be associated with oxen and horses. In old Lithuania the villagers showered their priest with handfuls of oats after he had finished the St. Stephen's Day mass — a custom not unlike the modern one of throwing rice at the bride and groom.

In England the day is known as Boxing Day. There the priest traditionally opened the poor box and distributed the alms to the widows and orphans of his parish. In the last few centuries it has also been the day when English families give "boxes" or gifts to those who have served them during the year — their maids, postmen, newsboys, and gardeners. In Central Europe this is a day for carolers to go around and receive goodies for their singing.

St. John

St. John's Day, or Third Christmas Day, December 27, is now almost forgotten, unfortunately. John is by far the most popular of the disciples, if we are to count churches named for him.

He seems to have died on the island of Patmos about the year 100, after a long exile from his position as bishop of Ephesus. According to legend the Roman authorities ordered him to drink a cup of poisoned wine, like Socrates. But John survived. Ever since, a glass of "St. John's wine" has been a mark of hospitality one offers to newlyweds, to travelers, and even to those lying on their deathbeds.

St. John's Day was considerably more popular than St. Stephen's. For one thing, it was a day further from Christmas and less buried in the shadows. For another, John's venerable age and his long exile on the island of Patmos made him a saint already during his lifetime. Furthermore, he seems to have been the only disciple to die a natural death. In any case, people tended to celebrate December 26th merely as Second Christmas Day, but December 27th not as third Christmas Day but as St. John's Day.

Holy Innocents

Holy Innocents' Day, December 28, recalls how King Herod slaughtered the infants of Bethlehem in his effort to kill the newborn Jesus, of whom the Wise Men had spoken. In the older tradition of the church this was a day when children ruled the roost, a joyous festival despite the rather gory paintings commemorating what had really happened.

At a very early period December 27th seems to have been the day not only of St. John but also of his brother James. December 28th similarly honored not only the Holy Innocents but also the death of Peter and Paul. These older celebrations tended to remain in the East, but alternate dates were chosen in the West. The reason for this is not apparent, except that the growing importance of Christmas in the West tended to crowd the other holy days to different times of the year.

THE NEW YEAR

New Year's Day is something of a hybrid, as is New Year's Eve, which fell on the day of St. Silvester—a bishop of Rome whose chief claim to fame was that he happened to be pope when Constantine proclaimed Christianity an official religion of the empire.

The ancient New Year was celebrated at a dozen different times in the year, even as recently as a thousand years ago. Not till the 1750s did it move to its present day, in the Anglo-Saxon countries. The Egyptians had once marked the new year when the Nile overflowed its banks, in May; the Romans, in March; the Greeks, in June; the Syrians and Russians, in April; the Jews, according to the Mosaic calendar, in March, though now in September or October.

Most of the celebrations connected with the new year are secular. Though the ancient custom was more to attend mass on St. Silvester's Night, or New Year's Eve, rather than New Year's Day, even this was not of ancient or of Roman tradition. As the 8th day after Jesus' birth, it was marked in France as the day of Christ's circumcision and naming, though these events seem not to have been celebrated in Rome.

In the time of Gregory the Great, January 1 was the Octave of Christmas, or the Octave of the Lord. The pagan gaiety and partying there were similar to the modern celebration of New Year's. After the time of Charlemagne the church attempted to soleminize the day by changing its name, which now became the Circumcision of the Lord. The Name of the Lord, or the Holy Name, was added still later.

The custom of churchgoing on New Year's Eve and New Year's Day is still popular in many churches — Roman, Orthodox, Anglican, Lutheran, Presbyterian, Reformed, Methodist, and others. Though the watch night services are not very liturgical but characteristic of American Methodism, they do attempt again what the church once strove for a thousand years ago—to change the mood of the day from excessive drinking and celebrating to quiet contemplation and worship.

To judge by the customs of ancient Gaul and the sermons of Asia Minor, the Christian New Year was invented chiefly to replace pagan orgies. St. John Chrysostom devoted his golden tongue to dissuade his people from the riotous banqueting and sexual excesses of the pagans. St. Ambrose wrote that the church had good reason to make New Year's a day of fasting.

New Year's Eve was traditionally a night of ghosts and spirits. In Northern Europe revelers wore animal skins, whirled in wild dances, and drank to the point of collapse. In the great forests of Poland and Russia peasants pounded on doors to drive out evil spirits. The modern counterpart of course is to shoot guns and beat pans.

In Austria the villagers carted special bells, specially consecrated by the priest, from cottage to cottage. The ringing was intended to ward off the evil spirits harboring there. These were also exorcized by the acrid smoke of burning straw.

In Puritan New England the New Year was the ideal time to ferret out witches. Though the Puritans would have been the last to admit it, witchhunting had been a part of Anglo-Saxon superstitions centuries before Christianity, and these pious people were merely perpetuating the ancient folkways under a cloak of faith.

Since the Reformation, Scotland has long had a good mixture of the religious and the secular. On New Year's Eve a good Scot first goes to church. Then he goes first-footing. Whoever is earliest to cross the threshold in the new year determines what kind of luck the household will have, especially when pretty girls are involved.

Dressing up as a mummer and going from door to door, usually as part of a group, used to be a religious custom. The most popular of these folk plays was that of St. George and the Dragon. Another was that of Galshan, a Scots version of St. George.

In New England the Pilgrims opposed New Year's nearly as energetically as they had opposed Christmas. No celebration, they thought, was preferable to a sinful one. In fact, they would not even put up with the name of "January." This of course came from the Roman god Janus, and they were convinced that they wanted nothing to do with a month named after a Roman deity. Instead they called it "First Month." To be consistent, they should also have changed the names of the days of the week, for these also commemorated pagan gods.

7

The Season of Epiphany

OLD CHRISTMAS

Epiphany now seems to be somewhat of an orphan as far as the Western church year is concerned, though at one time it was second only to Easter. To us it lies in the shadow of Christmas, though it is nonetheless the second great festival of the Christmas cycle, or in one of its older names, "Old Christmas."

Epiphany was of course at one time *the* Feast of the Nativity. According to the Egyptian calendar, which was 12 days behind the Julian one used at Rome, the winter solstice fell on January 6th, and the birth of Christ was tied in with the pagan festivals honoring the sun, exactly as was going to happen a century later with Christmas in the West.

In Asia Minor and Egypt it originally recalled not merely the appearance of Christ in human flesh — His Nativity — but several other historically distinct events: His baptism in the Jordan and the wedding at Cana.

The word *epiphany* means a showing, a manifestation, an appearance. Frequently the word represented the official visit of a prince or emperor. The root meaning came from "sunrise," or "dawn," and thus carried out the identical theme we saw in the Christmas Collects — Christ as the Sun of righteousness. In the Eastern church Epiphany was once a popular time to receive (baptize) new members — not called *catechumens* ("those who had been instructed") as in the West but *illuminandi* ("those who were to be enlightened," by Christ, the Light of the world and the unconquerable Sun).

Epiphany also bore such names as the Feast of the Manifestation, the Theophany ("Appearing of God"), the Appearing of Christ, or the Feast of Light. The reading from Isaiah (60:1) for the day still reflects its connection with light and with the sun: "Arise, shine, for Thy light is come."

In the East the mood of the day accented both Christ's incarnation and the beginning of His public ministry—first His baptism, as a kind of installation, and then the turning of water into wine at Cana, His first miracle. These events may have been stressed to counteract the growing influence of the Gnostics, who spurned anything material.

These Gnostics, or "Knowers," were an early sect who tried to "spiritualize" Christ's coming. They did not accept the claim that the Son of God was really *born* to His mother. They taught that the "birth of His divinity" began only with His baptism, i. e., when the Spirit descended upon the human Jesus. They would also have denied Christ's turning water into real wine, which did not seem "spiritual" enough to them.

By the middle of the fourth century, at least in the West, Christmas had begun to overtake Epiphany as the day on which the faithful remembered the Nativity. Rome celebrated both festivals but gradually changed the nature of Epiphany. About this time it also included in the pericopes the story of the visit of the Wise Men, perhaps because the legendary relics of the Magi had at that time been transferred from Constantinople to Milan.

THE WISE MEN

The story of the Wise Men must have been one of the most popular in the whole Bible, if we are to judge from second- and third-century mosaics, graffiti, and manuscripts. In art and legend these kings from the East made a colorful contrast to the drab shepherds and the humble manger. When the Mohammedans later overran the Holy Land, destroying churches as they went, they are reported to have saved one in Bethlehem solely because they looked up and saw painted on the walls men who were dressed as Easterners, like them—the Wise Men.

Only Matthew records the story of the Wise Men, and even he does not tell us half of what we should like to know. Oddly enough the pious legends that have grown up about them are now accepted as if on the same level with Scripture.

Augustine, Chrysostom, and other early writers mention the number of the Wise Men as 12. The Persian word *magi,* translated "wise men," really means "keepers of sacred things," "priest," "priest-scholars," or "astronomers."

Later tradition sets their number at three. Melchior, the king of Arabia, a Semite, was supposedly 60 years old; Balthasar, king of Ethiopia, a Negro, 40; Caspar, king of Tarsus, an Indo-European, 20. Their starting point was Babylon, according to the legends, and they made their way by camel up the fertile valleys of the Tigris and Euphrates, the standard route of the traders.

Matthew's account is more detailed concerning their visit to Herod than in any other part of the story. After following the star they arrived at the capital city of Jerusalem and naturally sought out Herod for the answer to their queston: "Where is He that is born King of the Jews? for we have seen His star in the East and are come to worship Him."

Already in the sixth century the Magi had come to be called "kings," though the expected term was Magi or Wise Men. Of the most ancient paintings, carvings, and statues, few show them with scepters, crowns, or royal robes until after the time of the Crusades.

Just when the Wise Men arrived at Bethlehem is not known. If the star appeared in the sky before Christ was born, they might have arrived on the night of his birth. If it first appeared on Christmas Eve, they could scarcely have arrived in less than two or three months. Herod, we know, decreed that the boys of Bethlehem up to the age of two were to be killed, and this may provide a clue to the time of their visit. Matthew says he did this "according to the time which he had diligently inquired of the Wise Men." Either he was playing the game unusually safe in killing so large an age group, or the Wise Men did not reach Bethlehem until a year or more after Christ's birth.

As the tale of the Wise Men grew, both in legend and song, their gifts took on symbolic meanings. Melchior is said to have brought the gold in a small casket or jewel box. Balthasar's frankincense was thought to be in a censer or thurible, and Caspar's myrrh, in a gold-encrusted horn. The gold was to represent Christ the King; the frankincense, Christ the Priest; and the myrrh, Christ the Prophet.

Eventually, according to the legends, the bodies of the Wise Men were discovered by the Empress Helena, mother of Constantine. From then on they were credited with a whole series of miraculous cures. For a time they were interred at Milan and later at Cologne, where they have long been a favorite shrine for pilgrims.

In Italy, France, and Spain the Wise Men are all but patron saints, certainly as far as the youngsters are concerned. It is the Wise Men who bring holiday gifts, not Santa Claus, and they appear not on Christmas but on Epiphany.

In Spain the day is known simply as *los reyes*—"The Kings." Everybody knows which kings are meant. The custom among children there is to place their shoes outside the home, filled with straw for the camels and with figs for the Magi's pages. In the morning the figs and straw have disappeared, and in their place the Wise Men have left gifts.

Many of the Epiphany customs are associated with water or with wine, as we might infer if we remember that Epiphany was once the day to celebrate Christ's baptism and the miracle at Cana. In the ancient lectionaries these readings had once been a part of the propers for the day, and Luther favored a return to the account of Christ's baptism, rather than that of the Wise Men. It seems strange that Christ's baptism is completely neglected in our church year.

In Palestine, the Jordan was naturally the site of a great procession and a blessing of the water. Elsewhere, too, streams and wells often received a religious blessing. The pious often drove their cows and sheep through such streams, carried home vessels of water from them, or dipped their crucifixes and statues in them. Water blessed on Epiphany was often given to the sick or sprinkled about the house.

Among the Greeks Epiphany is a day when the fishing fleet is blessed. The priest reads the Scriptures and then casts a crucifix into the water. A score of divers swim to recover it. The lucky one gets a handsome reward and the acclaim of all who are watching. This happy custom occurs not solely in Greece but wherever the Greeks have settled, especially in Florida and California.

In England the day was known as Twelfth Night, as in Shakespeare's play *Twelfth Night*. Among the English the day was a grand climax to the Christmas season, with huge feasts, banqueting, gambling, and reveling.

But under any of its names, Epiphany, Twelfth Night, The Feast of the Kings, Old Christmas, or the Baptism of Our Lord, the day was an important one. In the ancient church it ranked behind only Easter and Pentecost. Until 50 years ago it was a Roman Catholic day of obligation, as was Ascension. Since it usually fell on a work day, however, it was eventually disregarded, perhaps to conform more easily to the pattern of the American office and factory.

THE SUNDAYS AFTER EPIPHANY

At one time Epiphany had its own octave, which was often associated with the blessing of animals. Though the blessing has remained, the octave, alone of all the major and ancient festivals which had an octave, has now fallen by the wayside.

Until after the time of Gregory the Great the Sundays after Epiphany do not seem to have had any liturgical significance. They simply filled in the time between Christmas-Epiphany and Pre-Easter. In the oldest service books there were from 4 to 10 Sundays after Epiphany, but in the time of Gregory, with the growth of Lent and Septuagesima, the number varied from 1 to 6, depending on the date of Easter. The theme of the Epiphany season is the manifestation of Christ's glory in His ministry.

Generally the propers for these Sundays are similar in Roman, Lutheran, and Anglican uses, especially the Epistles and Gospels. Variations begin to occur with the fourth Sunday, where Introits and Graduals are repeated, and with the fifth and sixth, which are "wandering" days to fill in, if needed, at the end of the Pentecost season.

The Lutheran reformers, however, worked out a maximum number of propers from the ancient lectionaries for both the Epiphany and Pentecost seasons, to avoid the need for "wandering Sundays." They also appointed the last Sunday after Epiphany as the Feast of the Transfiguration. The Transfiguration was usually celebrated on August 6, but they considered it sufficiently important to fit it into the pattern of Sundays, since it normally would fall on a weekday and therefore be neglected.

CANDLEMAS: THE PRESENTATION

Another festival that occurred in the Epiphany season (unless Easter was unusually early) was the Presentation of Our Lord in the Temple, or Candlemas, falling on February 2. In the Eastern church this is known as "The Meeting of the Lord" (with Simeon and Anna), and in the Roman Catholic use, as the Purification of the Blessed Virgin Mary.

It commemorates the time when Mary presented herself and her Child at the temple, 40 days after His birth (80 days for a girl), according to the requirements of Lev. 12:2-8, so that the mother might be ritually cleansed and admitted once again to public services. A similar ceremony, "the churching of women" after childbirth, is still commonly practiced in England, though without any strict reference to a 40- or 80-day period.

This day — February 2 — also bears the familiar name of Candlemas. On this day or the following one (St. Blaise) the church once blessed candles for use at home and in the sanctuary, as the Latin church still does. The touching of the candle to the throats of the faithful was one of the church's more colorful "sacramental" blessings of the year, of the same rank as the crossing with ashes on Ash Wednesday or the giving of the fronds on Palm Sunday.

The story of the Presentation is one of the most appealing in Scripture. As the Holy Family enters the temple, the aged Simeon and Anna await the Child. The old people have been promised that they would see the Messiah before they die. Simeon's outburst of joy has found an esteemed place in the liturgy as the Nunc Dimittis: "Lord, now lettest Thou Thy servant depart in peace, according to Thy word, for mine eyes have seen Thy Salvation, which Thou hast prepared before the face of all people, a Light to lighten the Gentiles and the Glory of Thy people Israel."

In the earliest days of the church, Candlemas had more than its share of customs, often connected with light, candles, or weather. Some scholars think the church encouraged them chiefiy to replace the pagan commemoration at the same time of the year—how Ceres, Proserpina's mother, lighted a candle and searched for her, not knowing that the daughter was snugly in the underworld for the winter with Pluto.

The notion of Candlemas as an end of winter is also related to the Gospel for the day—the Christ who is the Light of the Gentiles now has physically returned with the growing daylight, much as if He were the Germanic god of spring, the God of Sun-day. This is of course the source also of the rather odd concept of Ground Hog Day, which tells us whether winter is really past.

8

Pre-Easter:
A Time of Preparation

PRE-EASTER (LENT)

Often when we celebrate such events as Advent and Lent, we imagine we are walking in the footsteps of the apostles. This is not true.

For the first century after Christ's death there seems not to have been a church calendar at all. Each Sunday was celebrated as a little Easter, and the chief festival was the wondrous period of 50 days between Easter and Pentecost.

Though the persecuted church began to develop a host of saints' days, even these were generally local and not so important that they could not be shifted to another date if the need arose. By the time of Irenaeus (d. 202), however, there seems to be some notion of the entire year as a picture of Christ's life and work. By the time of Augustine (d. 430) the church year had already come to be thought of in terms of "seasons" and "cycles," at least in a skeletal form.

In their primitive forms Advent, Christmas, and Epiphany made up the Christmas cycle, and pre-Easter, Easter-Pentecost, and the post-Pentecost seasons made up the Easter or Paschal cycle. Thus the whole church year mirrored what Christ had done and taught. This Christ-centered focus of the ancient church year was emphasized once again at the time of the Reformation, which dropped most of the saints' days to return to the ancient pattern of seasons and cycles.

The seasons of Pre-Lent and Lent are now frequently called Pre-Easter, a worthwhile change because it reminds us how the faithful, the penitents, and the catechumens joyously anticipated the coming of Easter. Down through the centuries the term Lent has taken on so many overtones of fasting and penitence that it somewhat disguises the true character of the season.

The proper mood is one of expectation, of waiting, not unlike that of Advent, in which the Christian ought to feel not only sorrow, because of his sin and Christ's death, but also joy, because of the triumph of His resurrection.

The first period is pre-Lent, from Septuagesima Sunday until Ash Wednesday. The next extends from Ash Wednesday until Laetare; the following one, from Laetare until Judica, also known as Passion Sunday. Then comes the Passiontide, from Judica until Holy Saturday. Within Passiontide there is Holy Week itself, which is further broken down into its lesser three days, Monday through Wednesday, and the Sacred Triduum: Maundy Thursday, Good Friday, and Holy Saturday.

The practice of fasting for Easter was known already to Irenaeus, who wrote the bishop of Rome about 100 years after the death of John: "Some people think they ought to fast for one day, others for two days, and others for even more; and still others reckon a time of 40 hours both day and night."

Irenaeus studied under at least one disciple of the disciples, and since he states that the fast was already exceedingly old, the practice may go right back to the time of Paul. If this be true, Lent, at least as a one- or two-day event, is as old as Easter.

Gradually Lent expanded until it included a 40-day period symbolizing the days Christ spent in the wilderness. Writers of the era of Augustine speak of Lent as if it were a 10th part of the year, 36 days, but the number 40 is more common—not including Sundays.

THE CATECHUMENS

Before Rome had become thoroughly Christianized, the weeks before Easter were the time when candidates for baptism received vigorous instruction and training, with baptism on Easter Eve. St. Augustine describes the confirmands as "harshly scourged with rules and instructions."

At the beginning of Lent those who wished baptism were publicly exorcised. The bishop admonished them to give up their allegiance to Satan. During this ceremony they stood barefoot on goatskins.

In this period of instruction the catechumens could not bathe or shave. They could eat only after sundown. If married, they lived in continence. Their chief occupation was meditation and contrition, often within the walls of a church or monastery.

On Passion Sunday they heard the Apostles' Creed for the first time, and on Palm Sunday, the Lord's Prayer. These came in a secret ceremony where they shook hands, promised faithfulness, and stated their desire to become members of the church. The rite was known as the *traditio symboli*. On Holy Saturday the confirmands were expected to "return" the symbol (the creed, or as some explain, the handshake that came with the creed) in a public examination. These "scrutinies" occurred several times during their instruction. The secret character of these instructions probably goes back to the age of the martyrs.

The Mood of Lent

Symbolically the 40-day period, not counting Sundays, parallels Christ's 40-day withdrawal into the wilderness. The Sundays bear distinctive names from the beginning of the Latin Introits: Invocavit (or Invocabit), Reminiscere, Oculi, Laetare, and Judica (often called Passion Sunday).

At one time these Sundays were probably known simply by a number, such as the "Fiftieth Before Easter," or in Latin, Quinquagesima. Quinquagesima does in fact fall on the 50th day before Easter, though the others were approximations. Septuagesima ("Seventieth"), Sexagesima ("Sixtieth"), and Quinquagesima, the three Sundays immediately before Lent, still bear their old names, though Quadragesima ("Fortieth") and those that follow now take their names from the Introits.

The oldest mood of Lent was not one of sorrow and sadness. The liturgies of the Eastern church, for example, retain the older Hallelujahs, looking forward to Christ's resurrection, though in the West the custom was to focus on His suffering and death. The accent on Christ's Passion in many Lutheran midweek Lenten services contrasts sharply with the more ancient lessons of the Sundays.

The mood of Lenten sorrow is marked by an ancient ceremony known as the "Farewell to Hallelujah." From Septuagesima on, the more joyous elements of the liturgy, such as the Hallelujah, the Gloria, and the Te Deum, were omitted.

In Hebrew *hallelujah* is simply a shout of joy, and like the word *selah,* it is not easily translated. Jerome tells us it was a kind of pious charm that fishermen sang while pulling in their nets, mothers while rocking the cradle, and farmers while wielding their scythes. Soldiers used it when attacking the enemy, according to the Venerable Bede, who tells of the Hallelujah victory of the Britons over the Picts in 429.

The quiet way to say goodbye to Hallelujah was in the liturgy, where the word was simply deleted; but there were also more sensational rites, in which the word was symbolically buried in a coffin or rolled up inside a straw scarecrow and burned.

Shrove Tuesday takes its name from "shriving," or the forgiving of sins. In many countries Shrove Tuesday is a time of reveling and celebrating before the great fast. It even gives us the word "carnival," the Latin for "goodbye to meat."

In the time of Charlemagne, fasting meant abstaining not merely from meat but also from dairy products such as milk, butter, and cheese. For this reason many a good housewife baked up what stocks of butter and milk she might still have into pancakes.

In French countries the day is called not Shrove Tuesday but Mardi Gras, or "Fat Tuesday." Perhaps this is because the housewife was expected to use up all her fats and butter in baked goods. Mardi Gras celebrations, like the great American variety in New Orleans, sometimes began as early as Christmas.

Rightly understood, the use of ashes at the beginning of Lent is an ancient and meaningful tradition, with roots going back to Bible times. Even Christ refers to ashes (Matt. 11:21). Until about the year 1000 the wearing of sackcloth and ashes was a sign of repentance for a gross and public sin — a murder, or unfaithfulness, or armed robbery.

Lent was the time when those who were guilty of public and serious sin publicly repented. This ceremony was even more austere than the one for the catechumens. Wearing coarse clothing, going barefoot, fasting, living in confinement (in a monastery or a cave), the penitents, one by one, were led into the church, sprinkled with holy water, and touched with the ashes. Then they read the seven penitential psalms.

At the time of the Crusades the use of the ashes became popular for all the faithful, not just for public penitents. Even the priests were marked on the forehead with the ashes, often in the form of a cross. The ashes usually came from the burning of the year-old palms saved from Palm Sunday.

Lenten fasting at one time served a useful and Christian purpose. Fasts were common in Biblical times. In the New Testament period the church encouraged the faithful to fast on those days when Christ died (Fridays) and when Judas agreed to betray him (Wednesdays). The food which would normally have been eaten during a fast was given to the poor.

Today fasting has almost disappeared as the requirements have lessened even within the Roman Catholic Church, especially since Vatican II. Luther and other reformers were not opposed to fasting as such, provided it was a preparation for the proper reception of Communion. As the Scriptural reading for Ash Wednesday makes quite clear, however, outward preparations are far less essential than inward ones.

Foods such as pretzels and hot cross buns stem directly from Lent. At the time when the fast was far stricter than it is now, including a ban on dairy products as well as meat, as it still does in Eastern Orthodoxy, people subsisted largely on breads and pastries, eked out with soups and vegetables.

Pretzels are one of these Lenten foods. Bakers in Germany decided to turn out something that even looked religious. The crossed arms of the pretzel were intended to represent a Christian at prayer, with his palms on opposite shoulders making a crisscross of his forearms. In Latin the shoulder was known as the *bracella,* and through the German this eventually gave us the word "pretzel."

Hot cross buns as we know them today probably are too rich in shortening to have passed muster in the fasting laws of the Middle Ages. What we have now may have developed from small loaves of bread, marked atop the crust with the sign of the cross. A similar kind of bread, sweetened a bit with shortening and sugar, is still common in Spain and Portugal as a special treat on any kind of religious occasion — Christmas, Easter, a christening, a wedding.

In Germany, despite the great tradition that made sacred music a central part of public worship, all singing was dropped during Lent. When Johann Sebastian Bach was at Leipzig, for example, the organ and the choirs were silent during these weeks, with music coming back into its own for Palm Sunday and Easter.

Occasionally, however, in accord with the general mood of sobriety, a violinist or soloist did perform during Lent, usually in a minor key. Maundy Thursday and Good Friday often featured great choral presentations of the Passion, such as the St. Matthew Passion.

Like Easter, the English word "Lent" got its name from the folklore of the Germanic tribes. "Lencten" is the same root as "lengthen," and stands for that time of the spring when the daylight does in fact lengthen.

LAETARE

Even within the season of Lent there are distinct moods and accents. Laetare, the Fourth Sunday in Lent, breaks into the general mood of self-denial in the same way that Gaudete, the Third Sunday in Advent, breaks into the season of Advent. On this Sunday the Roman church permits rose as a liturgical color.

The Epistle for the day speaks of Jerusalem as "the mother of us all," and from this reading the Sunday is often known as Mothering Sunday. Originally this was a day when children returned to their home churches and to their families.

On this day the pope often gave special recognition to those who had upheld the faith in a significant way. When he awarded the Golden

Rose—a filigree rose of worked gold— to King Henry VIII of England, he also granted the king the title *Defender of the Faith,* largely for his writings against Luther.

PASSIONTIDE

Passion Sunday, the Fifth Sunday in Lent, also known as Judica, marks the beginning of Passiontide. This season is older than Lent and focuses on the Passion. The chants for these days contain many ancient hymns that describe Christ's suffering, such as *Vexilla regis, Pange lingua,* and *O Sacred Head, Now Wounded* (of Reformation origin).

The Scripture readings also begin to take up the theme of the crucifixion. Traditionally this was also the day when the cross disappeared beneath a veil, together with all statues and pictures, not to reappear until Easter.

The feeling of awe that surrounds Lent influenced even church architecture. Massive rood screens of stone and wood began to hide the mystery of Christ's sacrifice from the eyes of the faithful. In the East the screen became a solid wall, and the priest was as effectively sealed off as if he had been officiating within the holy of holies.

HOLY WEEK

Holy Week largely reflects what the church at Jerusalem once did. In the first two or three centuries Jerusalem was not only the most ancient but also the most influential of the ancient bishoprics, and citing the example of the place where Christ suffered and died was the strongest possible argument one could raise for imitating it.

The Spanish pilgrim Silvia, or Etheria, who journeyed there about the year 390, has given us a detailed description of the liturgy at Jerusalem. She writes not only about Easter, Epiphany, and Pentecost but also about the new churches Constantine built there. Her description of Holy Week and Easter is probably the clearest and oldest we have.

By the time of her visit Helena, Constantine's mother, had completed churches at the traditional sites which were hallowed by Christ's life—where He was born, where He died, where He celebrated His last supper, where He raised Lazarus. To these sites the faithful had long made pilgrimages.

By Etheria's time the pattern was already rather elaborate. On the Saturday before Palm Sunday the Christians first gathered in Bethany at the church built in honor of Lazarus. The next morning they trooped to the church at Golgotha, built to honor the martyrs. In the afternoon they worshiped at shrines on the Mount of Olives.

Before the crowds left the Mount of Olives, they listened to the account of Jesus' entry into Jerusalem. Waving palm and olive branches, they marched triumphantly toward the city. The bishop, as a type of Christ, rode on a donkey, and the faithful ended each hymn with the refrain: "Hosanna to the Son of David. Blessed is He that cometh in the name of the Lord."

At dusk, on Maundy Thursday, taking food along, they withdrew for the night to the Mount of Olives, where Jesus had prayed with His disciples. At dawn on Good Friday they trudged off to the courtyard of Pilate to hear the Evangelists' accounts of the trial.

Etheria cites various "stations" of the cross, including those at the court of Pilate, at Calvary, and at the Holy Sepulcher. Unfortunately she skips over the activities of Holy Saturday by commenting that they did not much differ from those in Spain, probably centering on the liturgy of the sacred fire and on the night-long vigil.

She does mention other customs, largely those of Easter and the Octave of Easter. Those who have spent an Easter in modern Jerusalem will note that many of them have not changed at all, whether the worshipers be Orthodox, Roman, Syriac, Coptic, or Amharic. She especially noted the service on Easter night, which recalled Jesus' return to the Upper Room, and that of a week later, which commemorated His encounter with Thomas.

Those who have studied Silvia's account are convinced that the rites at Jerusalem (and perhaps other Eastern patriarchates) strongly influenced those of the entire church. Pilgrims who made the sacred journey to Jerusalem were often of high rank, and once they had experienced these customs in Jerusalem, introduced them into their own areas. The rites involving Palm Sunday, the veneration of the cross, the procession of candles from out of the tomb, and the open-air reading of Scriptures all stemmed directly from Jerusalem.

PALM SUNDAY

Christ's triumphal entry into Jerusalem is a pleasant interlude in a week of suffering and death. Almost universally it bears the name Palm Sunday, though in parts of central Europe it was also once known as Blossom Sunday or Willow Sunday, probably because palms were unknown there. What those who welcomed Christ into Jerusalem once waved were probably palm and olive branches, together with a sprinkling of spring flowers. Exactly this same kind of pathway — flowers and leaves — is still often laid in Spain and Portugal not only for a Palm Sunday procession but for any parade, for instance, one in honor of a visiting head of state.

To a Semite the palm has always been a tree of honor. It marked the place where he could find water for his flocks. Its very name in Hebrew—Tamar—was a favorite one for a firstborn daughter. Outside a cemetery in Cairo or Beirut even now you will find not flower stands but ancient crones selling palms—palms to place on the graves, palms to symbolize eternal life.

The story of Christ's entry into Jerusalem historically falls on Palm Sunday, though liturgically it belongs to the first Sunday in Advent. The readings for Palm Sunday, or Second Passion Sunday, continue the account of His suffering and death. The blessing of the palms comes from the period of Alcuin and Charlemagne. The reformers generally omitted the blessing of the palms on the theory that people were to be blessed, not things, but they did not discourage the use of unblessed palms.

In Jerusalem the practice had been to accompany the bishop into the city with palms and marching songs. One famous hymn that developed in Europe from the Palm Sunday parade goes:

> All glory, laud, and honor
> To Thee, Redeemer, King,
> To whom the lips of children
> Made sweet hosannas ring.
> Thou art the King of Israel,
> Thou David's royal Son,
> Who in the Lord's name comest,
> The King and Blessed One.

This was written down by the Bishop of Orleans, Theodulf, who lived at the time of Charlemagne. Sometimes these primitive songs were rather funny, at least to modern tastes. A stanza of this hymn that we no longer use has been translated in this fashion:

> Be Thou, O Lord, the Rider,
> And we the little ass;
> That to God's holy city
> Together we may pass.

In the rural backwaters of Europe the Palm Sunday parade is still traditional, in part because it happens to come at the time of the year when nature is awakening and the sun is warm and people are in a festive mood. In some places a wooden figure of Christ and the donkey were once mounted atop a cart or wagon and drawn to the market square by all the young men. En route the priest sometimes paused to sprinkle holy water over the graves.

After the services and pilgrimages of Palm Sunday, the housewives of the parish set about spring cleaning. In the oldest rites this appears not so much a house-cleaning as a church-cleaning. In the country parishes of England one can still see with how much pride the village women wash the walls, wipe off the cobwebs, and scrub the floors — that God's house may sparkle for Easter.

Although an annual spring cleaning is not so much a part of our life now as it was in the days of our grandmothers, when coal fires made it almost a necessity, the custom does have religious roots. The Mosaic code demanded that the house had to be perfect for the Passover, and many Christian women kept up the pattern set by the Ruths and Marthas and Marys.

In general the Monday, Tuesday, and Wednesday of Holy Week held no great significance, though in many country towns special fairs, Passion plays, and other semireligious activities were held. The country people who had come to town for Palm Sunday often stayed until Easter, lodging with relatives or in barns.

Among youngsters a fairly common practice was a trip to a sacred well or spring. There the youngster threw a pin or a stone into the water, to clarify it, and returned the next day to drink. Frequently children flavored the water with Spanish licorice, and in some hamlets "Spanish Day" was the most common name for Palm Sunday.

MAUNDY THURSDAY

The name for Maundy Thursday is so ancient that there is some doubt what "Maundy" really means. Most scholars suppose that it is a late Latin corruption for the word *mandatum*, "commandment." Then "maundy" would refer to the instructions Christ gave His disciples: "A new commandment I give unto you that ye love one another." Other likely possibilities are the Latin word *mundo*, "to wash," referring to the footwashing, or the Saxon *maund*, "basket," referring to the distribution of money and food to the poor.

In some countries Maundy Thursday means not only communing in one's church but also a ceremonial meal in one's home, recalling the Passover Jesus shared with His disciples. Often the Old Testament custom of eating lamb, wine, flat bread (matzoth), and a bitter herb (horseradish) sets the pattern, especially when it can serve as a teaching device for children.

Like many other Christian festivals, Maundy Thursday had a great variety of names. One of the commoner ones was Chare Thursday or Sheer Thursday, meaning "clean." This refers to the ceremony of scrubbing the altar. At Avignon and Arles, where Christianity once flourished in an even more mystical form than at Rome, the day was known as the Birthday of the Chalice. This name recalls how loyally the French revered the legends of the Holy Grail, the chalice Christ used in the Upper Room.

In Germany the day is known as *Gründonnerstag.* This probably comes from an ancient German word *grunen,* meaning to mourn. By folk etymology, however, it came to mean "Green Thursday," since at one period green had been the color of the vestments for the day.

Three masses were authorized on Maundy Thursday. The first began at sundown on Wednesday evening, in the pattern of a vigil, and was variously known as the Mass of Remission, Tenebrae, or Black Matins. After the penitential psalms the candles were extinguished one by one until the whole church lay in darkness.

At this time the public penitents, who had been preparing themselves by fasting and meditation all during the Lenten season, prostrated themselves, received absolution, and were granted once more the right to share in the Communion.

Of the masses in daylight hours the first was for the consecration of holy oils, used in such rites as baptism, exorcism, confirmation, the anointing of the sick, and the ordination of priests. This was of course performed by the bishop.

The third mass, the one in the evening, commemorated the institution of the Lord's Supper. Duchesne, one of the greatest of liturgical scholars, points out its ancient origins by citing several characteristics of this mass which no others had: it broke into the ancient cycle of weekday Communions otherwise held only on Wednesday and Friday; it offered the Sacrament to the faithful at night (since 1952 this general prohibition has been relaxed); it offered the Sacrament at a time when the faithful had not been required to fast.

Because of the joyous nature of the Lord's Supper on this night, the Roman Catholic vestments are now white, though Lutheran and Anglican churches generally use violet, the usual color of Lententide. At one time green was also common. The church bells ringing during the Gloria further mark the joy of the day, though these then hang silent until Easter.

In the early centuries foot washing was one of the most popular customs of the year, even in Rome, where the pope faithfully washed the feet of all comers. In England, however, foot washing remained a lively rite. In return for a year's obedience and loyalty, a king's subjects could expect at least one boon—a ceremonial foot washing. Cranmer speaks of it as an ancient and beloved ceremony.

In England the king not only washed feet but also "made his

Maunds" — distributed food, clothing, and money from a *maundy,* or wicker basket. Often the custom was to minister to as many pensioners as there were years in the king's age.

The ceremony began as the king washed, wiped, and kissed the feet of those who had been chosen as the most needy in the parish. Next the Royal Almoner distributed shoes, clothing, food, and money. Specially minted coins were one of the most picturesque elements of the rite, valuable collectors items which are still a mark of the Maundy Thursday celebrations in England.

Not all kings and queens were enthusiastic about foot washing. Queen Elizabeth I, for example, thought it beneath her dignity to wash anyone's feet and assigned the task to her ladies-in-waiting. She did stoop, however, to paint the sign of the cross on each foot, once the washing had been accomplished. Another relic of this ancient attitude appears in the little nosegays the clergy carried — to ward off the disease and plague they once feared when they came in contact with the poor.

GOOD FRIDAY

Good Friday has almost as many different names as Maundy Thursday. One of the common ones in northern Europe was *Karfreitag,* as it was known in Germany, or Care Friday, as it is still occasionally termed in northern England. *Kar* and *Care* mean sorrow, or mourning. Long Friday, Great Friday, Holy Friday, or as in the ancient church, Preparation Day *(Parasceve)* were other common names.

The word "good" in Good Friday may refer to the great good that God accomplished for mankind on that day, but more likely it represents a vowel shift from the older form of *God's* Friday. The change from God's Friday to Good Friday would exactly parallel the one from *"God* be wi' ye" to *"Good*bye." In any case linguists closely link the words *good* and *god* and are convinced they were once the same word.

Good Friday was so sacred and awesome that the vestments of the priests were black, that no candles were lighted, that the altar remained bare, and that no mass was celebrated. Christ was ritually buried behind the stone altar, the place in the ancient churches of Italy and Greece and France where saints' relics were buried. In the Roman Catholic Church the day has been made one degree less somber in recent years in the new rite allowing the faithful to commune on Good Friday, as on other days when mass is said, with elements consecrated the day before.

In the centuries before the Reformation, Good Friday often began with Black Vespers late on Maundy Thursday. After readings from the Old Testament and the Gospel came the Bidding Prayer — a long general prayer made up of "bids," or petitions, for "all sorts and conditions of men"—one of the oldest forms of prayer known to the church.

Other readings were known as "reproaches," in which Christ symbolically took the faithful to task for their unfaithfulness, interspersed with hymns such as the *Pange lingua*. Next came the reverencing of the cross. Under the supervision of the clergy, the cross or crucifix was taken down from the altar or the reredos and laid upon the steps of the chancel. The whole parish then proceeded to kneel in turn before the cross, paying it obeisance with a kiss.

During the long Good Friday rituals, which at least in the more ancient tradition did not include a celebration of the Eucharist (in Lutheran circles communing on Good Friday seems to have been common only in those areas which were strongly influenced by the Calvinists), another popular element was the reading or chanting of one of the Gospels in its entirety or a Passion history made up from the accounts of the four Evangelists. Sometimes the leading roles—Christ, a narrator, John the Baptist, Peter—were played by a team of deacons or servers.

This custom of the ancient Church of Rome came to life again in medieval Germany in musical form. When Bach composed the St. Matthew Passion, assigning the leading parts to singers and supplying hymns for the congregation, he was merely doing in polyphony what once had been done in plainsong. Especially in Lutheran lands—Germany and Scandinavia—listening to the sacred music of Bach or Schuetz remains one of the most moving and popular ways of setting aside Good Friday.

A Good Friday custom of quite recent origin is the *Tre Ore*. This service became common in South America and Italy in the 18th century. Centering on the seven last words of Christ, including also hymns and prayers, the "Service of Three Hours" recalls the time Christ hung on the cross.

As a day for processions, Good Friday had few equals, especially in the sunny lands of the Mediterranean. In Portugal a straw or wooden image of Judas Iscariot is dragged through the streets and ceremonially hanged. Often he is beaten with brooms and pelted with stones and in Mexico even shot with guns. In Greece, villagers throw cracked pottery at him. For good measure, they also call down on his head all the curses they can remember.

Spain boasts some of the most colorful Holy Week pageantry in all Christendom, still living in the primitive splendor of the medieval world. The *Semana Santa* climaxes with the great processions of Good Friday, especially in Seville, Granada, and Malaga. Here the pageant of the Passion, featuring such leading characters as Pilate, the Virgin,

Jesus, Mary Magdalene, Peter, John, and Judas, reminds one of the famous play at Oberammergau.

Often these processions include a door-to-door collection for the poor and an unending hullabaloo on drums and kettles and tambourines. The plaintive chants go back to the time of the Vandals and Visigoths, some scholars say, and the sad words and tunes are not unlike the Spanish *flamenco* or the Portuguese *fado*.

In Italy all who marched in the parade, monks and townsfolk alike, wore a crown of thorns. In England villagers tolled the church bells on Good Friday. There a full set of bells numbers nine and is often called the Nine Tailors (tellers). First the bells rang out nine times to indicate that the one who had died was a man (six for a woman, three for a child), and then 33 strokes to indicate how old Christ was.

Holy Saturday

Holy Saturday, also known as Great Sabbath or Sabbath of Glory, reflects the quiet of the Jewish Sabbath and particularly Christ's rest in the tomb. It was an important day of fasting; not even the weak and children were excused.

Generally there were no services during the daylight hours of Holy Saturday, though by the 14th century some of the rites anciently appointed to the Easter Vigil, which began at sundown, were transferred to an earlier time of day. Since 1955 the Roman Catholic Church has once again returned to the older use.

Holy Saturday marked the day when the catechumens reached the final stage of instruction and preparation. Usually they gathered in the church in the afternoon, with men on one side and women on the other—a pattern which could be found in some American churches as recently as a generation ago.

The catechumens were once more exorcised against the powers of Satan, and their ears and noses were touched with holy chrisms. Facing the West, each of them in turn recited: "I renounce you, Satan, with all your pomp and works," and facing the East: "I dedicate myself to you, Jesus Christ, eternal and uncreated Light."

In the last hours of daylight the catechumens were left alone to meditate and pray, awaiting along with all the faithful, the Vigil of Easter—when they would be received in Baptism and would share in the Eucharist.

9

Easter — The Feast of Feasts

The Vigil

At dusk on Holy Saturday, lamps and candles blazed out across the countryside in churches, homes, and shops to mark the beginning of the Easter Vigil — the greatest service of the Christian year. Even the public thoroughfares gleamed with light, we are told. At Milan, Emperor Constantine once ordered so many torches lighted that people claimed the night was even brighter than the day.

Easter Eve had such names as the Night of Illumination, the Service of Lights, or the Night of Radiance. This was the night when the Paschal candle was blessed and lighted, a symbol of Christ as the Light of the world. On this night those who were to be baptized, the *illuminandi* (those who were to be enlightened), assembled with the faithful to celebrate Christ's resurrection.

The symbol of light was central to the joyous celebration of Easter, even as it was to Christmas. The ancient hymn "Hail, Gladdening Light" *(Phos hilaron)* was one of many that marked this service, and century after century the image of Christ as the Sun has carried right through Easter hymns, as in the Scandinavian "Like the Golden Sun Ascending."

Already in the third century Tertullian comments that the Easter vigil lasted throughout the night, with readings of Scripture, antiphons, and prayers. Toward midnight those who were to be baptized stripped themselves of jewelry, listened once again to the final exhortations of the bishop, marched to the baptistry, and stepped into the water.

There the bishop baptized them, first the men, then the women and children. After being anointed with one of the oils specially consecrated on Maundy Thursday, the *illuminandi* donned fresh white linen tunics and new sandals. These were the garments they wore for the whole octave of Easter, giving a special name to the Sunday after Easter — White Sunday.

In the Easter procession the clergy, those who had just been baptized, and all the other faithful gathered up the sacred vessels and lectionaries, left the church by a side door, marched around the church-yard, and ceremoniously knocked at the main door of the church – which was locked and closed, to represent Christ's tomb. With the swinging wide of the doors and the chant "Christ Is Risen" the whole assembly then reentered the sanctuary for the service of the Easter Eucharist, usually just before dawn.

After the sixth century, however, when the great majority entered the ranks of the faithful through baptism as infants rather than as adults, the numbers of baptismal candidates shrank so drastically that the baptismal liturgy began to fade out of the Easter vigil.

The notion of the Easter fire, however, never did disappear. When the church was completely dark and there was no sound except the rustling of service books and vestments, the priest struck a light from flint and steel and with his "new fire" touched a candle, sometimes the Paschal Candle. Often the candles of the faithful were also lighted; the new fire was then taken home in tinderboxes to kindle fresh flames on the hearth.

The symbolical bursting out of light in a world of darkness re-presented the coming of life out of death and Christ's victory over the world of darkness, a splendor as bright as the Easter sunrise. This whole symbolism was one of the most moving ones in the ritual of the church.

In Jerusalem the striking of new fire in the Church of the Holy Sepulchre has been one of the most enthusiastic and emotional rites any church can experience. Right down to modern times the fire almost magically bursts from the tomb of Christ and travels by ship and plane to half the Orthodox churches of the world. During certain periods of the Middle Ages the excitement got out of hand. Worshipers crowded too enthusiastically in upon the priests; scores were trampled or burned to death right inside the basilica.

The custom got so out of hand that the Easter Vigil was banned, at least in those churches which paid allegiance to Rome. Today however, the new Easter rites once more authorize this custom, minus the wild enthusiasm one often finds among the Orthodox.

The Paschal Vigil, as it was once known, had many ties with the Jewish Passover, also known as the Feast of Unleavened Bread, or *Pesach*. It recalled the days of Pharaoh and the plagues, when God's people were rescued from death by the blood of the paschal lamb on their doorposts.

Today it is difficult to imagine how the early church, beset with persecution and martyrdom, could be so carried away by Easter. Yet the mood of the faithful was continually one of *hallelujah,* not of *miserere.*

THE DATING OF EASTER

The dating of Easter, as we saw in an earlier chapter, was for centuries a confused issue. The East argued that it should fall on the 14th of Nisan, no matter what day of the week this turned out to be. The West argued that Easter should always fall on a Sunday, regardless of the date of the Passover.

This was one of the chief issues at the Council of Nicea in 325. To keep local bishops from establishing their own dates and to bring order out of confusion, the council persuaded Constantine to send out a letter designating Easter as the first Sunday after the first full moon after the spring equinox.

The council did not want Easter to coincide precisely with Passover. If the first full moon fell on a Sunday, Easter would be postponed one week.

Even today, the dating of Easter in the churches whose background is Syriac, Greek, Russian, Egyptian, or Ethiopian still differs from that of the West. The Orthodox usually celebrate one to four weeks later than the West, though the difference now is not one of principles but of calendars—the Gregorian versus the Julian. Even as late as the time of George Washington, the American colonies still used the old Julian calendar—a proof that the confusion about the dating of Easter is not really so ancient as we like to imagine.

EASTER CUSTOMS

As the oldest and most revered day of the church, Easter has accumulated the largest number of customs and legends—rabbits, chicks, eggs, lambs, clothing, parades, lilies, and ham. By origin many of these traditions are pagan. These the church reinterpreted. Even the name of Easter is pagan, meaning simply springtime.

The word for Easter in the lands of southern Europe was almost always a derivative of the Hebrew *Pesach,* or Passover—*Paques, Pascoa, Pascua,* or *Pasqua.* The northern half of Europe learned to call it Easter.

All across the face of Europe the customs of the spring festival lingered on, either under the name of Pasch or Easter. Now the task of the faithful was to Christianize them. The giving and the coloring of eggs, for example, had long been a rite of spring. Now it assumed new meaning.

The chick and the egg now represented not only the gift of new life in nature but also the Christian belief in life bursting the walls of death in Christ. Along the shores of the Aegean, church members began to paint their eggs with Christian symbols—a fish, whose Greek name represented the Savior, or a Chi Rho, the beginning Greek letters of the name Christ.

Sometimes eggs were baked whole into the crust of bread. Passed round to one's friends, they were a sign of common faith. Often as not they were painted red—some say to stand for the blood of Christ, the color of the sun, new fire, or even martyrdom.

Fire, of course, has long been a part of Easter. Dating back to the days of St. Helena, mother of Constantine, Orthodox Christians have every year brought the holy fire back from the Church of the Holy Sepulchre in Jerusalem. Eventually the fire from Jerusalem is carried as far away as Leningrad and Nicosia and Constantinople and Addis Ababa. Even in far-off England, in the country villages, it is considered good luck to strike new fire with flint and steel every Easter, to get spring off to a proper start.

Sprouts and seedlings are also common symbols of Easter, especially along the Mediterranean. When Christ said that a grain of wheat must first be buried in the earth and die before it can sprout and bring forth fruit, he was applying it both to Himself and to others. In Naples those who come to church on Easter are given a seedling of wheat to remind them of Christ's rising.

During the Middle Ages Easter parades and plays were common in every churchyard and on every village green. Inside the church, altar boys took the role of the three Marys and acted out the story of the women arriving at the empty tomb. Games, dances, contests, and feasts followed, turning Easter into one of the biggest days of the year.

Sometimes gifts were exchanged, such as the elaborately jeweled eggs of gold that were so popular among the Russian czars. To keep up the holiday mood, villagers often took turns ringing the church bells. Children sometimes dared to spank their parents if they could catch them still in bed at sunup.

In Greece and Russia the common greeting at Eastertide, "Christ is risen," was always met with the equally joyful response: "He is risen indeed." Everyone was allowed to give "a holy kiss" to anyone he met. Though this has largely died out in communist Russia, it is a joyous reminder of the real meaning of Easter. The Austrians have extended this Easter exuberance throughout the year when they greet one another daily with *Grüss Gott,* God bless you."

The origin of the Easter parade lies buried under centuries of tradition. Four or five hundred years after the first Easter the Byzantine emperors, whether at Constantinople or Ravenna, encouraged their courtiers to wear their finest garb for Easter. This had also been a custom at Rome in honor of the return of spring.

Today the clothing stores and fashion houses have commercialized this old custom until we can hardly recognize it. New York's annual Easter parade is a good example. What began as a leisurely stroll from the stately old parishes of lower Manhattan has now become a fashion parade.

Fifth Avenue hosts so many poodles in mink coats, actresses leading baby elephants, and publicity men flaunting the latest creations that the pleasant old custom of wearing new clothes for Easter is buried under gimmicks and dollar signs.

Egg rolling and all the other games played with eggs probably date at least from the Middle Ages. In England bishops, priors, and priests mingled freely with the people on the common, knocking hard-boiled eggs together to see whose could stay uncracked the longest.

The church suggested that egg rolling symbolized the rolling away of the stone from Christ's tomb. Whether or not this was the real origin, egg rolling proved to be great sport. The eggs that were broken could always be eaten, along with other food. After the long Lenten fast, the country folk were proud to eat up the stock of eggs they had stored away, boiling them lest they spoil.

Egg rolling came to America from England and Germany and like many another custom, became Americanized. Nowadays there are variations such as egg coloring contests, Easter egg hunts on horseback, and even egg throwing.

By far the best-known of the egg rolls is the one in Washington. Back in the days of Dolly Madison the site was the Capitol lawn. Eventually it moved to the White House, though many a president or his lady refused to have little urchins trampling on their grass and roses.

Nowadays the children bring their own eggs and roll them down the White House slopes. Only children are admitted, or parents who are accompanied by a child, and a lively business has sprung up among some youngsters who for a quarter will "take in" some stranger as their dad and then go back for another! But this is all in the best spirit of childish enterprise.

Eating ham for Easter seems to be an English custom. Perhaps the reason is the same as that for eating eggs—to break the fast. After six weeks of meatless, eggless meals, anyone with a few spare shillings in his pocket celebrated by eating as well as he could.

The choice of ham rather than beef or mutton was probably of pagan origin. The pig had long been a symbol of good luck and prosperity, as any child knows when he puts his pennies into a piggy bank. One of the greatest delicacies a Hungarian or Pole can order is roast suckling pig. Thus Christians continued to eat ham in the springtime, even after they were converted.

In our age we tend to smile at some of the confused customs of our forefathers, who sometimes mingled the superstitious and the religious. Yet we often do the same thing, sometimes without realizing it. At Natchez, Miss., for example, there is an Easter sunrise service on top of an old Indian mound. This is not strange, perhaps, until one realizes that these mounds were once places of burial for those who worshiped the sun and the moon. A modern Christian does not really believe in a sun god — he just chooses the same place to worship.

In America Easter did not become a major festival until after the Civil War. Except in churches with a strong liturgical background, like the Episcopal, Lutheran, Roman Catholic, or Eastern Orthodox, Easter differed little from any other Sunday. In New England the Puritans were death on street fairs and egg rolling, or even on Easter hymns. Except for the reading of the Easter story, there was no festival, nor was there a festive meal. And New York was scarcely different, at least when sturdy Dutch governors like Peter Stuyvesant made every Sunday colorless and joyless.

What really established Easter in America was the Civil War. When a huge number of her young men fell under the guns of Gettysburg, Vicksburg, and Atlanta, America suddenly found herself in need of Easter. Christ's resurrection became a symbol of *our* resurrection. Easter became a day of solemn mourning, a day when we remembered the war dead.

Much of the credit for establishing Easter in America goes to the Presbyterians. Though these sons of John Knox did not retain nearly as much of the church year as they had known in Scotland, it was they who conducted many of the public Easter services in places of importance and influence — in the halls of Congress, in state legislatures, in war cemeteries.

One of the liveliest of Easter traditions is the "Easter Duty." In England, and to a lesser degree in other parts of Europe, the difference between a Christian and a non-Christian is that the Christian "does his Easter Duty." He goes to church. He receives Communion. And in this quiet way he testifies that he believes in Christ's resurrection and in his own.

One of the common problems among parents, in this day of hunting for Easter eggs, is how to relate Easter to children. Eggs are no problem, especially if we remember how the ancient Christians exchanged eggs.

The rabbit is somewhat more difficult, though it represents *ongoing* life even in a world of death.

Singing Easter carols is one of the finest ways of teaching what Easter is all about. The child can learn much from hymns like "Jesus Christ Is Risen Today," "I Know That My Redeemer Lives," "The Strife Is O'er," "The Day of Resurrection."

Some families like to bake an Easter cake representing the Lamb of God, a custom that is common in Germany and Scandinavia. Painting religious symbols on hard-boiled eggs (a fish, a dove, a Chi-Rho, an Alleluia, or a Pax) is easier and often far more attractive than merely dipping them in color.

Many a youngster enjoys lighting a special candle, perhaps at the dinner table. This of course is a reminder of the ancient Paschal Candle lighted in so many churches, reminding us that Christ is the Light of the world. In medieval days a candle was usually lighted from one in church and then carefully carried home to light the hearth and cook the Easter meal.

THE EASTER SEASON

The mood of Easter did not end with sundown. All through the week the newly confirmed wore their white linen and attended services. Missals of France and Spain in the time of Charlemagne indicate that two or three services were held every day. The feast lasted not merely through the octave but right on for 50 days until Pentecost.

All six Sundays after Easter, along with Ascension, belong to the Paschal feast, though they also look forward toward Pentecost. Most of these take their names from the Latin words of the Introit.

Quasimodogeniti, the First Sunday After Easter, gets its name from the verse: "As newborn babes, desire the sincere milk of the Word." The day is also known as Thomas Sunday, White Sunday, Low Sunday, and the Octave of the Passover.

Misericordias Domini, the Second Sunday After Easter, takes its name from Psalm 33:5: "The earth is full of the goodness of the Lord"; *Jubilate,* the Third, from Psalm 66:1: "Make a joyful noise unto God, all ye lands"; and *Cantate,* the Fourth, from Psalm 98:1: "Oh, sing unto the Lord a new song."

Rogate, the Fifth, breaks the pattern, taking its name from the Rogation Days during the week of the Ascension. Another name for the day, *Vocem iucunditatis,* follows the usual pattern in taking its name from the Introit, Is. 48:20: "With a voice of singing declare ye." *Exaudi,* the Sixth and the bridge between Ascension and Pentecost, gets its name from Psalm 27:7: "Hear, O Lord, when I cry with my voice."

10

Pentecost —
The Great Fifty Days

THE SEASON

The 40 days from Easter to Ascension, along with the 10 from Ascension to Pentecost, were days of such spiritual excitement that the disciples celebrated them with as much joy as they did Easter.

The church fathers often referred to the whole period as Pentecost, meaning 50 days, without restricting the name to a single day. Throughout these days, sermons, readings, prayers, and hymns reflected the mood of thanks and praise, with no echoes at all of the gloom of Good Friday.

The Council of Nicaea in 325 specifically banned any kind of kneeling during Pentecost. Kneeling, they said, was a mark of penitence and humility. The faithful were to pray boldly, standing upright. For the same reason the council outlawed fasting.

This mood of Paschal joy did not at all harmonize with the Rogation Days, the three days before the Ascension, which began to develop late in the fifth century. When the Council of Orleans formally sanctioned the Rogationtide in 511, many authorities at Rome refused to accept them, on the grounds that so historic a time for *Hallelujah* should not be tempered with three days of *Lord, have mercy.*

ASCENSION

Ascension and Pentecost were such close links in the same chain that they were originally celebrated together, usually on Pentecost. Christ Himself showed how they were joined (John 16:7; Acts 2:33). As Chrysostom put it, both observances show that "we who appear unworthy of God's earth are now taken up with Him to heaven." In Jerusalem the church first celebrated the Ascension not on the Mount of Olives but in the basilica at Bethlehem, to show that in His earthly nature Christ was still flesh of our flesh and to link the beginning of His earthly life with its end.

The fullest account of the Ascension appears in the Acts of the Apostles. Here we read how Christ gathers His disciples round Him, charges them with proclaiming the Gospel, promises that He will send the Holy Spirit, and then ascends to sit at the right hand of His Father. Two angels appear, asking: "Men of Galilee, why do you stand looking into heaven? This Jesus, who was taken up from you into heaven, will come in the same way as you saw Him go into heaven."

As soon as Christianity had become a lawful religion within the empire, Helena, the mother of Constantine, made concerted efforts to pinpoint those places in the Holy Land that were associated with our Lord's ministry. One of these was the Mount of Olives. Helena built a church there at the supposed site of the Ascension, though the building was several times destroyed by Arabs and Syrians. This basilica was thought to enshrine the very stone on which Christ last stood, and the pious believe His footprints are still visible.

Easter, Ascension, and Pentecost were once the three most important festivals of the church. Of late, Christmas has probably surpassed all three, at least in Western Christendom. Now it is Ascension that goes unnoticed. In America only the liturgical churches still have services on Ascension — and even most Lutherans and Episcopalians are barely aware of the day.

In France and Germany Ascension was a popular day for a pilgrimage to a shrine or holy hill. Here the townsfolk acted out the events of the day. In some churches a statue of Christ was symbolically pulled up through a hole in the roof.

The Paschal candle, as a symbol of Christ's presence with His people, was solemnly extinguished. Now Christ would be present no longer in a visible manner but would instead send the Holy Spirit.

Ascension seems to have been a specially important holiday among the Crusaders. The Knights Templars honored it with special reverence, and many a crusader emblazoned the symbols of the Ascension on his armor and pennons.

One common symbol of the Ascension is the lion and the dragon. The lion represents Christ, ascended in triumph to His Father. The dragon represents the devil, allowed once more to battle for the souls of men.

Exaudi

Exaudi, the Sunday between Ascension and Pentecost, has the same characteristics of joy, hallelujahs, and praises that mark the other five Sundays after Easter. The propers make no mention of the ascended Lord. In many uses this day was simply called the Sixth Sunday After

Easter, though the medieval Roman name was the Sunday Within the Octave of the Ascension.

PENTECOST

The climax of the whole Paschal season is Pentecost. On this day we commemorate the outpouring of the Holy Spirit on the disciples. Pentecost's ancient importance, like Epiphany's, is demonstrated by its Greek, rather than Roman, name.

In the Old Testament the Jewish Pentecost was known as the Feast of the First Fruits, the Feast of Weeks, or the Feast of the Harvest. Originally it was a thanksgiving for the harvesting of the wheat. Later it also recalled the giving of the Law on Mt. Sinai, as a kind of "birthday" of the Jewish religion, and was also a day on which all male Jews were commanded to bring their tithes to the temple.

The Book of Ruth with its accounts of farming and gleaning and family life, was the appointed Scripture for the day. Today it is popular as a time when a Jewish boy holds his bar mitzvah, when he is given the responsibility to observe all the commandments.

As good Jews the disciples probably would have gathered in Jerusalem to celebrate the Jewish First Fruits even if Christ had not told them that He was sending them His Holy Spirit. Luke describes what happened on this day in considerable detail—the sound of the rushing wind, the tongues of fire, and the speaking in foreign languages.

In English-speaking Christianity Pentecost often goes by the name of Whitsunday. White of course was the color of the robes worn by those who were baptized on that day, either because they had missed the ceremony at Easter or because the rivers were still too cold then.

Later there was also an allegorized explanation. In Anglo-Saxon, *wit* or *whit* means wise, or wise man, or elder, as in the word *witenagemot,* a council of elders. Therefore it used to be customary to speak of those who had been baptized as those who had been made wise—wise unto salvation, of course.

Except for the baptismal service on the Eve of Whitsun, there were few special liturgical observances. The vestments for the day were often red, to recall the tongues of fire that settled on the disciples. Elaborate hymns to the Holy Spirit also developed, largely between the time of Charlemagne and the Crusades. The most famous of these is probably *Veni, Sancte Spiritus* (Come, Holy Ghost, in Love).

Like Good Friday and Easter, Pentecost adopted many customs which were not originally Christian. Most of these were rites of spring—dancing round the maypole, decorating the house with foliage, playing courtship games.

The church tried to counteract some of these nature rites with drama. The story of Pentecost was often acted out in the church, a fine method of teaching in a day when few could read. Churches in France often released a dove from the ceiling of the nave, to symbolize the descent of the Holy Spirit.

In Germany red rose petals dropping down through a hole in the roof represented the tongues of fire, and trumpets furnished the sound of the rushing wind. In Bohemia pious villagers sometimes went so far as to drop burning straw from the roof beams, as tongues of fire, but the bishops ordered this stopped after several churches went up in smoke.

As an antidote to the frequent moral excesses of Pentecost, Luther preached that the joys of the day ought to be those of the spirit and not of the body. The selling of ale by the medieval church on this day brought in a huge amount of money, but it also encouraged drunkenness. Some monasteries sold beer and wine in such quantities that the profits from the octave of Pentecost supported them for the other 51 weeks of the year.

Colonial America knew Pentecost by its Dutch name—*Pinkster.* Among Negroes this was a major holiday. Masters often gave the slaves as much as a week of freedom, and the days were marked with traveling from one plantation to another, buying new clothes, singing, dancing, and downing barrels of rum.

The Greek Orthodox have a service of penance and sorrow on the closing night of Pentecost. At this service the priest and his deacons dress in somber black, and encourage people to end their pagan celebrating and repent of any excesses committed during the 50 days of festivity.

Because Pentecost had so many ties with spring, it was especially popular in rural areas. The dew in the meadows was considered a magic potion against all sorts of disease, and at dawn many peasants were abroad, walking barefooted through the grass.

To protect their animals, farmers often put out pieces of bread to soak up the moisture and then fed them to the stock. Before the Christian era, people stayed up all night, banging on pans, cracking whips, and ringing bells. These rites were to scare the evil spirits away from one's cottage and fields. Otherwise one's house might catch fire, his wheat be eaten by weevils, or his cow die of milk fever.

In areas of Europe that are largely rural, such as Spain and Portugal, the Sundays between Easter and Pentecost are still days of special rejoicing. Villagers take turns preparing simple banquets for their friends and neighbors.

The Holy Ghost takes a prominent position at these feasts, usually in the image of a silver dove or a crown. The custom has become so popular that villagers build special wayside "Holy Ghost chapels," which are not really churches but places for a party.

In various corners of Europe Pentecost is known as Flower Festival or Green Holiday. In Italy it is Red Easter—*Pascua Rossa*.

In the time of Charlemagne the whole week after Pentecost was considered a time for celebration, not just the single day. During this week farmers were forbidden to harvest their hay, bricklayers to put up a chimney, shoemakers to cut hides. Later a council decided that three days of celebration was enough—a decision that was probably intended to cut down sensual excesses.

Whitmonday is still a holiday for most Europeans. Today it is mostly a time for picnics—in fact, the hymn "Onward, Christian Soldiers" was written for just such a picnic. The Rev. Sabine Baring-Gould wrote it so that his schoolchildren would have a good marching song as they paraded off on their Whitmonday picnic.

Unfortunately Pentecost is no longer the holiday it once was, probably because the drinking and love-making that sometimes accompanied it almost killed it as a church festival. Pentecost still ought to be a red-letter day in the calendar of the church, reminding us that Christ left us on this earth to carry out His will and to be the earthly temples of the Holy Spirit. This is what Pentecost is really all about and how it ought to be celebrated.

11

The Season After Pentecost

CYCLES AND SEASONS

Even though the Christian year came about largely by accident, its growth was not completely haphazard. The first half of the year ran from Advent through Pentecost, stressing the life of Christ, and the second half, His teachings. This pattern emerges clearly from the early sacramentaries and missals; it seems to have resulted naturally from the great festivals of Christ in the first half of the year and the displacement of many saints' days to the second half.

In a stricter sense the entire church year has to do with the life of Christ. The first "cycle" of the first half includes Advent, Christmas, and Epiphany; the second, Lent, Easter, and Pentecost. In the second half of the year, that which follows Pentecost, the lessons focus on Jesus' teachings and on the Spirit and His work among us.

This was such a long season that further attempts were made to break it up. The common dividing points fell at the end of June, in mid-August, and at the end of September, with the feasts of SS. Peter and Paul, St. Lawrence, and St. Michael.

With its fondness for symbolism, the church of the Crusades even assigned a meaning to each of these four periods. That from Pentecost to the Feast of SS. Peter and Paul represented the apostolic age. That from Peter and Paul to St. Lawrence represented the age of persecution. That from St. Lawrence to St. Michael represented the church at work in the world today. That from St. Michael to Advent represented the church triumphant.

In this fashion of counting, a given Sunday was known not as the Sixteenth Sunday After Pentecost, or the Fifteenth Sunday After Trinity, but the First Sunday After Michaelmas.

In the Eastern Church the custom was to count only from Pentecost. Pius V standardized this method of counting in the Roman Catholic ordo only in 1570. The Anglicans retained the system they had known in the Sarum use, and the Lutherans the Mainz use, counting the Sundays from Trinity.

Liturgically, Pentecost is far more significant than Trinity. Pentecost is an event, and Trinity is a doctrine; all the ancient festivals recall events rather than doctrines. The service books of many European Lutherans have now returned to the older custom of dating the Sundays from Pentecost, though they often retain as a secondary title the Sunday "After St. Lawrence," or "After the Apostles."

Generally the propers for the Pentecost season remain reasonably similar among the Western churches, though to a lesser degree than those of the first half. This becomes easier to understand if we remember that the propers for this season were not finally fixed in the Roman Catholic Church until 50 years after the Reformation.

The dislocation of some of these propers from one day to another came primarily from the insertion of new ones for Trinity Sunday. These pushed the Epistle, the Gospel, the Introit, or the Collect a week out of line.

In general, again, the Epistles and Introits for the season more frequently fall on the same day than the Gospels and Collects. The Gospels are usually no more than a week apart, but because of a further Anglican dislocation of the Collect it is possible, starting with the Fourth Sunday After Pentecost, to hear the identical Collect one Sunday in a Roman Catholic church, the next Sunday in a Lutheran church, and the third in an Episcopal church.

Trinity Sunday

Trinity Sunday is certainly not an ancient holy day, perhaps because the doctrine of the Trinity was always taken for granted. Tertullian tells us that already in the second century devout Christians were making the sign of the cross with three fingers, representing Father, Son, and Holy Ghost. This was a standard ritual scores of times daily — before one ate, drank, bathed, left the house, climbed into bed.

Invoking Father, Son, and Spirit was normal for any act of worship, for any blessing. In the days of the Arian heresy, which questioned whether Jesus was wholly God, the Trinitarian invocation was written out in full in the missals and lectionaries — previously it had been presumed — so that no one could publicly be a crypto-Arian.

During the decades when the Franks overran Gaul, the bishops considered the doctrine of the Trinity so important, especially for new converts, that they set aside a special day for it. By the 9th and 10th centuries those who did not observe Trinity Sunday were treated as outcasts, almost as heretics. The day was a favorite among the courtiers of

Charlemagne and of his chief religious adviser, Alcuin. In 1334 Pope John XXII named it a holy day, fixing the date as the Sunday after Pentecost.

The doctrine of the Trinity has always intrigued and puzzled the church. Over the years hundreds of symbols have come to represent it — on stone, glass, canvas, and plaster. The figure of the deer or hart, for example, which had long represented Christ, now appeared as three deer enclosed in a circle.

More popular symbols were the shamrock, the trefoil, the triangle, interlocked circles, and the fleur-de-lis. Occasionally the triangle was surmounted by an eye — the figure on the back of an American dollar.

Because Trinity developed as a major holiday at the same time Europe was reeling from the plagues, the invocation of the Trinity often became a kind of folk magic to ward off disease. Many a church or monastery was the result of a vow, when town or noble promised God a building if He spared them from the plague.

In central Europe "Trinity columns" went up after almost every epidemic. Vienna boasts a dozen such monuments, thankofferings by those who were spared. The pillars were as popular and as ornate, in their day, as war memorials are in ours.

Minor Festivals of the Lord

The mood of the Pentecost season — of the new life in the Spirit — does not end with Pentecost or Trinity. It lingers on until the last Sunday or two before Advent. In fact the church year is a little like the epistles of Paul — which first tell us what God has done for us and then what we should do in response.

Once there were frequent minor festivals of the Lord also during the Trinity season. Perhaps unfortunately, these have almost gone by the board. Hardly any of the churches celebrate them any more, not even the Orthodox. Among Roman Catholics, Lutherans, Anglicans, and Protestants generally, they are little more than interesting antiquities.

From the English custom of marking important dates on the calendar in red and lesser ones in black, these festivals are sometimes known as black-letter commemorations of our Lord. They include: The Finding of the Cross, The Transfiguration, The Name of Jesus, and Holy Cross Day.

The Finding of the Cross, along with Holy Cross Day, though originally two distinct events, are really so close in mood that they were often celebrated together. They recalled the legendary finding of the cross by St. Helena and the building of the Church of the Holy Sepulcher.

The Feast of the Transfiguration, most commonly celebrated on August 6th, seems to have been one of many celebrations the Crusaders brought back. The Latin Church now celebrates the Transfiguration on the Second Sunday in Lent. Anglican reformers once dropped it from the calendar completely, though it has gradually worked its way back. Among the Lutherans Bugenhagen plumped for the Last Sunday After Epiphany.

Both for spiritual and doctrinal reasons the Transfiguration is important. Why the Anglican reformers considered it "popish," since it had good Biblical support from three Evangelists, is hard to understand.

The most recent of these black-letter festivals of the Lord is The Name of Jesus. This recalls the appearance of the angel to St. Joseph, saying "Thou shalt call His name Jesus, for He shall save His people from their sins."

Anglicans celebrate it on August 6th, Roman Catholics on the Second Sunday After Epiphany, and Lutherans on January 1st, together with the Feast of the Circumcision. Doubtless the development of the Holy Name societies and the devotions written by St. Bernard (d. 1153) did much to popularize it, including his hymn:

> Jesus the very thought of Thee
> With sweetness fills the breast;
> But sweeter far Thy face to see
> And in Thy presence rest.

REFORMATION

Reformation falls on October 31st, the day Martin Luther posted his Ninety-Five Theses on the door of the Castle Church in Wittenberg in 1517. Normally the Reformation is celebrated on the nearest Sunday, not on a weekday. Lutherans have been celebrating the Reformation since the 16th century, along with many of the Reformed, who of course also recall the work of Zwingli, Calvin, Knox, and Melanchthon. Only in the last century, however, has the Reformation become a day the majority of American Protestants remember.

Briefly, the Reformation commemorates Luther's challenges of medieval aberrations in doctrine and practice. In the Ninety-Five Theses he especially attacked the system of indulgences and the plan of salvation they implied. In those days indulgence was a broadsheet, sold by itinerant monks at a considerable price, which assured the buyer that God had forgiven him his sins, future as well as past.

Unfortunately, the common people imagined they were buying forgiveness and in some cases considered the documents they bought a license to go out and sin. Stung rather severely, the church soon recognized the dangers of such money-raising methods and has never again returned to selling indulgences.

At first Luther intended no more than posting on the bulletin board a few pages of Latin theses that he wished to debate with his colleagues, but in effect he drove a wedge right through Christendom. Within the space of three or four years most of his fellow Augustinians, many parish priests, and the great majority of German Christians sided with Luther.

Although there were also other great events in the story of Luther — the burning of the bull, the speech at Worms, and the writing of the Augsburg Confession — the posting of the theses was the first significant act of the Reformation — an event which shook Germany, and in fact all Europe. Only Rome's massive Counter-Reformation in the second half of the 16th century managed to save half of Europe for Latin Christianity.

The Reformation accomplished almost as much good within the Roman Church as in the churches of the Reformation, because it evoked major reforms within that group. At the Council of Trent that church mapped out and authorized its own reformation. Furthermore, the age of discovery, the growth of nationalism, and the birth of the printing press brought fresh insight and thought to the whole medieval world, including also the church, which in many respects had grown insular and secular.

A proper celebration of the Reformation, however, should not be a negative one, a mere matter of finding fault with the church as it existed in the 16th century, but a positive one, according to which we thank God for the many gifts He has restored to His people — the Scriptures, salvation by grace, preaching, hymns, the freedom of the individual conscience, the universal priesthood of all believers. These had been present in Christianity from the very beginning, but they had been partially buried under the dust of centuries until they were rediscovered by the Reformation.

HARVEST AND THANKSGIVING

Of all the holidays in the church year, none is so distinctively American as Thanksgiving. This is not to belittle the harvest festivals of other countries. Yet nowhere else is the day quite so festive; nowhere else is it such a rich combination of religion and patriotism.

Already in the Old Testament, God had commanded His people to celebrate His bounty. In Canaan, with its semitropical climate, there were two harvests, one in the spring and one in the fall. The Jews called the spring festival the Feast of the Weeks, and the fall festival the Feast of the Tabernacles. These are described in considerable detail in Deuteronomy 16 and in Leviticus 23 and 29.

Notions of harvest and the ingathering were a natural part of many of the saints' days, depending on the season. Thus St. Anne's Day in Italy was the time for gathering melons, as was St. Michael's Day in France for grapes, and St. Andrew's Day in England for apples. Local parishes also frequently held a harvest festival in connection with the anniversary of their church's consecration, which was often conveniently held before winter set in.

European harvest festivals often stemmed from pre-Christian times. In Switzerland a pretty girl played "the bride of the harvest," with heads of wheat plaited into her hair. Sometimes there was a "harvest doll," woven of wheat straws in the shape of a baby, borne aloft through the main street. These of course were relics of ancient fertility rites honoring Ceres, the goddess of grain.

The best known of the harvest festivals was St. Martin's Day, November 11th. What Americans call Indian Summer Europeans call St. Martin's Summer. In Holland a pious family is apt to have a big dinner of roast goose and new wine, both traditional for the day. Since huge meals were not common in English harvest festivals, the Pilgrims likely learned about feasting when they lived in Holland.

The first American Thanksgiving was that of the Pilgrims in 1621. During the previous winter, with little but bark shanties to keep out the snow, 43 of the 100 souls who had sailed over on the *Mayflower* died —a dreadful toll.

But now the crops had flourished and the Indians had taught them how to protect themselves against the weather. Governor Bradford ordered four men to go out and bring back geese, ducks, turkey, and partridge.

Meanwhile others combed Cape Cod for fish, oysters, and clams. Chief Massasoit and his braves got wind of the feast and brought four deer. Ninety Indians eventually joined the three-day Thanksgiving, but in any case there was ample food, complete with games and contests.

One odd part of the first Thanksgiving was that it did not seem to include a church service or prayers, despite its name. That element seems to have developed later.

In England thanksgiving usually marked a special event—a king's recovery, the birth of a prince, a military victory, or the end of a plague. One of these thanksgivings occurred on Guy Fawkes Day, when Guy had tried unsuccessfully to blow up Parliament.

In 1622 the Pilgrims did not celebrate, but in 1623, this time in the summer, they did. This Thanksgiving seems to have had minor religious overtones, though generally the Pilgrims were convinced — for a century, at least — that worshiping God and making feasts were not compatible. The second Thanksgiving marked both the *Anne's* safe voyage from the Netherlands and the end of a summer's drought. From then on, Thanksgiving occurred sporadically throughout New England for a century but was only of local importance.

In 1789, after the Revolutionary War, George Washington proclaimed a national Day of Thanksgiving, and so did President Madison after the War of 1812. In the South there remained a notion that Thanksgiving was somehow Yankee, and it was rarely celebrated.

Thanksgiving as we know it on a set day and as a national observance doubtless dates from the proclamation of Abraham Lincoln in 1863. The President got the idea from Mrs. Sarah Hale, editor of America's leading women's magazine, *Godey's Lady's Book*. For decades Mrs. Hale had poured out editorials, petitioned governors, and written to presidents, encouraging an annual day of thanksgiving.

Partly because of the disruption of the Civil War, partly because of the great toll of the Battle of Gettysburg, Lincoln set aside the fourth Thursday of November as a day of national humiliation and thanksgiving. He was careful to use words which would not embitter the South, and within a decade Thanksgiving had become a nationwide festival.

Oddly enough, though the Pilgrims were otherwise extremely religious, the Thanksgiving ordered by Lincoln was far more religious than that of the Pilgrims. Now Thanksgiving was not just a day of feasting but also of churchgoing. Today wherever Americans live, even if in some far-off corner of Asia or Africa, as missionaries, diplomats, soldiers, or businessmen, Thanksgiving has become one of the most American and most popular of all our holidays.

The End of the Year

The last Sundays of the church year have a character that is somewhat different from the others of the Pentecost cycle. The Lutheran reformers provided propers for a full 27 Sundays after Trinity, but the Roman Catholic use was to provide them for only 23 (24, counting from Pentecost). The Anglicans offer 25.

If Easter falls unusually early and propers for the additional Sundays after Pentecost are required, they are borrowed from the "wandering" Sundays — the series not used at the end of Epiphany because Easter fell early.

The mood of these final Sundays is one of Christ's second coming and of His judgment, along with the end of our earthly life. The readings reflect the pattern of an older time when Advent began much earlier than it does now, perhaps as early as St. Martin's Day, November 11.

The last Sunday after Pentecost, in Lutheran use, often commemorates the dead, as it does in much of northern Europe. Doubtless the reformers wished to keep the occasion of All Saints' Day and All Souls' Day but wished to do away with many of the unscriptural practices connected with these holy days.

12

Saints and Martyrs —
The Cloud of Witnesses

THE AGE OF THE MARTYRS

Most Protestants, especially the American Protestants, know very little about the saints. Perhaps this is the influence of the Reformation. Calvin, Knox, Luther, Cranmer, and Zwingli all discouraged prayers to the saints.

The mere mention of the word "saint" makes many a Presbyterian, Lutheran, Methodist, or Baptist see red; he hesitates to call even the Evangelists *"Saint"* Luke or *"Saint"* Mark. Luther was as well aware as anyone that the veneration of saints, especially by those who understood their faith but little, sometimes crowded Christ out of the picture. And yet even he kept in his study a statue of the Virgin Mary, explaining that it helped remind him how Christ became flesh of our flesh.

One cannot deny, however, that the reverencing of martyrs was one of the oldest elements of the church's calendar. To worship Christ under Nero, Domitian, or Diocletian often as not meant a sentence of death. Many of the Roman emperors were quick to make examples of those who refused to pour out a cup of wine or light a cone of incense before the statue of the Caesar. This religious act was looked on as an oath of loyalty in an age when the emperor was worshiped as God.

The more common modes of execution were by wild animals, by gladiators, by beheading, or by burning. Once a Christian had died, however, his debt was paid. The state respected his body and yielded it to his family or friends.

Though every Christian was constantly under threat of death, the persecutions were sporadic. For long periods the church could worship freely, and those who gathered in homes or caves quietly were not bothered.

As early as three or four decades after the death of Jesus the tombs and sarcophagi of the martyrs apparently began to be used as Christian altars. Psalms, Scriptures, creeds, and even the Eucharist were read over their coffins. Christians gathered annually at the tombs, usually on the anniversary of the martyr's death. With the single exception of Easter, these days of the martyrs are the oldest festivals of the Christian year.

Both in the New and the Old Testament the term "saints" at first meant nothing more than the people of God, whether living or dead. In the oldest sense all believers are saints.

Some of the saints and martyrs are mentioned in the Scriptures, for example, James, Stephen, and the Holy Innocents. As the numbers of martyrs grew, the early church began to keep lists, and we still have such lists dating from the time of Emperor Constantine.

Though the early church gave distinct honor to all who gave good testimony to their faith, it had a special place of honor for those who gave up their lives – the martyrs. Others who kept the faith under imprisonment or torture were known as confessors. Another category, as the listing of the saints developed, was that of the apostles. And after the period of the persecutions, any good Christian of remarkable life and faith could be declared a saint.

Except for festivals of major saints like John the Baptist and the Virgin Mary, saints' days normally recall the day of death, not the day of birth. This was called the saint's *natalitia,* or heavenly birthday.

At first the reverence for saints may have been nothing more than a pious recollection, not unlike what a mother does when she visits the grave of her son and places flowers there, though it eventually consisted of a service over the tomb.

Generally the recollection of martyrs was local. St. Martin, for example, was highly thought of in France, and St. Nicholas, in Asia Minor. Only with the passing of several centuries did the observance of local saints' days begin to spread throughout the empire, and then almost always from East to West, with very few of the Western saints ever making the calendar in the East.

With the passage of time, of course, many of the stories about a given saint turned to legend. In fact, saints like St. Margaret, St. Blaise, and St. Nicomede may be completely legendary, without any historical prototype at all.

In the last century Rome has searched through the pedigrees of many of its saints, chiefly through the scholarly Dutch order of the Bollandists, and has quietly suggested that no more churches be dedicated in their honor and no more children assume them as patrons.

The veneration of saints spread rapidly after Constantine's Edict of Toleration in 313. With the building of new basilicas and with the church no longer in the catacombs, the relics of the martyrs were often transferred. Frequently, as was probably the case with the martyred Peter and Paul, their new name day came from the date of the reburial, especially when the date of their death was in doubt.

THE MARIAN FESTIVALS

The festivals that center on the life of the Virgin Mary are not typical of those of other saints or of martyrs, but they do show how saints' days multiplied. Right down through the centuries the poor Virgin has been both praised and maligned, as pious legends began to grow into doctrines.

Both Roman Catholic and Eastern Orthodox theologians are the first to admit that although in the early church the Virgin was highly revered, her place of honor was somewhat less than that of Paul, Peter, or John.

In the early centuries the church was so often referred to as Mother Church or the Virgin Mother or the Bride of Christ that there was sometimes a confusion in terminology between the church and Mary. France, "the oldest daughter of the church," and the one that supplied the greatest number of holy days, was especially fond of the term "Mother Church," and scholars have noted it in letters from Lyons and Vienne within a hundred years after Christ's death.

Already at the end of the second century the church fathers were concerned with the Virgin Mary. Tertullian denied the legend that she had never consummated her marriage with Joseph, arguing against the Gnostics that her physical relationship with Joseph was an added proof of Christ's human nature. Origen cited the Biblical reference to Jesus' "brothers" against the Docetists, again emphasizing Christ's human nature.

On the other hand, little more than a century later both Augustine and Jerome upheld the doctrine that she was perpetually virgin, though Augustine would not go so far as to say she was without original sin.

The cult of Christ's mother received its main formulation at the Council of Chalcedon in 451. There Mary was formally declared *theotokos* ("Mother of God") and perpetually virgin.

Today there are as many as 17 days in the Roman calendar dedicated to Christ's mother. Five are major, the rest, minor. Two of the major ones, though long "held in pious hearts," did not become a part of Rome's official calendar until the 20th century. The five major Marian festivals are: the Purification, the Annunciation, the Nativity, the Immaculate Conception and the Assumption.

The festivals of the Purification and the Annunciation give few Protestants any trouble when they are properly understood. At first these holy days seem to have been celebrated more as events in the life of Christ than of His mother.

THE PRESENTATION — FEBRUARY 2

A good Episcopalian or Lutheran, or perhaps even a Methodist or Presbyterian, knows the feast of Purification as the Presentation of Jesus in the Temple. This is the day when Mary and Joseph first brought the infant Jesus to the temple.

According to the law of Moses, every Jewish mother was to present her firstborn son 40 days after his birth, dedicating him to God. Luke tells us just how Mary and Joseph did this and how the ancient Simeon and Anna came to meet the newborn Savior. A relic of this pleasant Jewish rite is still common in England. In what the Book of Common Prayer calls the "churching of women," the mother goes through a similar ritual of prayer and thanksgiving at the birth of every child, including those who are girls.

The ancient names for this day clearly show that it was a holy day honoring Christ rather than His mother. Like the Annunciation, it falls into the first half of the church year — the half that is traditionally known as the year of the Lord and marks the major events in Christ's life, not in the half given over to the saints. In the churches of Syria it was known as the Presentation of the Lord in the Temple, in Greece, as The Meeting of the Lord, to mark the day on which He met Simeon and Anna.

By the sixth or seventh century the festival was common throughout the empire. In Rome it helped replace the torchlight processions of the Lupercalia, from which it borrowed many customs. In the ancient legends the goddess Proserpina spent each winter with Pluto in the underworld, where she could be warm and safe from the blasts of winter. Each spring her mother faithfully set out with candles to seek her. This is probably the source of the common name for the day — Candlemas.

This day also is intertwined with the folklore of Groundhog Day. If the groundhog sees his shadow, there are to be six more weeks of winter. Some scholars feel that the groundhog was thought of as Satan, and the sun as Christ, the Dayspring from on high. When Satan sees Christ, he once again scurries into his burrow.

During the Middle Ages rich Roman noblemen brought huge candles to the Lateran, where the pope blessed them and distributed them to the poor, who could not afford candles and had to spend the winter in darkness. The custom fell into ill repute as the poor fought, argued, and trampled each other.

In many countries the faithful bring along large and decorated candles to be blessed. These they use throughout the year as sacramentals, burning them at the bedside of one who is seriously ill, at the home altar, or at a wedding party.

The Annunciation — March 25

The second of the Marian feasts is the Annunciation or Visitation. This falls on March 25, exactly nine months before Christmas, and marks the visit of the Angel Gabriel to the Virgin Mary to tell her of the great miracle God had in store for her.

Because Christmas was long celebrated on various dates, so was the Annunciation. The ancient names of the day, like those of the Presentation, also indicate that it was more a festival of Christ than of the Virgin: The Conception of Christ, The Glad Tidings to Mary, The Annunciation of the Lord. Mary's great hymn of praise, the *Magnificat,* is often closely associated with the Annunciation though more properly this should be noted in a distinct holy day known as The Visitation of Mary to Elizabeth.

Like most of the Marian feasts, the Annunciation was late in coming to Rome, even though the bishop there was first among peers and the arbiter in doctrine and liturgy. Duchesne, the great French liturgist, feels that all the Marian feasts were borrowed from the Byzantine missal.

In some parts of the church March 25 was also thought to be the day on which the Lord was crucified, the day on which God created Adam and Eve, and the day the Jews were freed from Egypt. In Hungary and Austria the day became known as Swallow Day. In America, at the same time of the year, the swallows return each spring to the old Spanish mission at San Juan Capistrano.

Besides the Presentation and the Annunciation there are three more major holy days connected with the life of Mary: the Nativity, the Immaculate Conception, and the Assumption.

The Nativity of the Virgin — September 8

The Nativity of course refers not to the birth of Christ, Christmas, but to the birth of Mary. It seems to have originated in Syria or Palestine. There it was celebrated on September 8, which was also the day to commemorate Mary's parents, Anna and Joachim.

By the seventh century it was well known throughout Italy, and by the eleventh, throughout Christendom. One French bishop preached about it in the seventh century as a "new" holy day. For 1100 years it was a holy day of obligation among Roman Catholics, but it was downgraded again as recently as 1918.

Traditionally Mary's birthday was also a harvest festival. September was the time for the grape gathering, and Mary was a patron of the winemakers, perhaps because of her role at the wedding at Cana. In the Alps this was often the day when peasants drove their cattle down from the mountain before the snows began.

The Marian feasts least accepted among Protestants are the Immaculate Conception and the Assumption. Both of these are relatively recent, and seem to have become popular in the West in spite of all that Rome could do to stop them.

THE IMMACULATE CONCEPTION – DECEMBER 8

The Immaculate Conception's oldest name in half a dozen European tongues was The Feast of the Normans. Celebrated on December 8, this festival came to Western Europe through the Norman Knights who in the 11th century conquered much of the old Byzantine empire. The Crusaders were especially fond of feasts to the Virgin, perhaps because of their code of courtly love, and brought back from Constantinople, Nicosia, Damascus, and Jerusalem many of the devotional practices they found there.

The Immaculate Conception of Mary is distinct from the Virgin Birth of Christ. To a Roman Catholic, Mary was conceived normally by Anna and Joachim but was in a miraculous way preserved by God from the guilt of original sin. (Incidentally, John the Bapist is also thought to be free of original sin.)

This gives Mary a status somewhat higher than that of other human beings. She could be guilty only of actual sin, not of inherited sin. Yet it also keeps her a step below her Son. The idea of the immaculate conception, of course, was to guard her Son from inheriting original sin, since He inherited His human nature from her.

Many Western theologians did not accept these innovations about Mary's immaculate conception, for example, St. Anselm (1033 – 1109) and St. Thomas Aquinas (1225 – 1274). Aquinas said he had no complaint if the Eastern Church wished to celebrate it but thought it had no place in the West. Both Anselm and Aquinas have been formally canonized, of course, which certifies their writings as free of error. At the time of the Reformation, the Immaculate Conception was an optional feast, depending on the desire of the local bishop.

During the 17th and 18th centuries the influential lead of Spain and of France brought it more and more into prominence throughout the

Roman Church. In Spain, where Mary was the patron saint, local celebrations included festooning the church with flowers, holding first Communions, staging processions, and giving pageants.

In 1854 Pius IX officially made it a day of obligation, despite the objections of numerous bishops. Since that edict, for Catholics at least, it has evolved into one of the most important days of the year.

THE ASSUMPTION — AUGUST 15

In point of development the last of the great Marian feasts is the Assumption, or as it is called in the Book of Common Prayer, The Falling Asleep of the Blessed Virgin Mary.

In pious tradition, as distinct from doctrine, the Assumption is one of the older festivals of the church, but as an official day of obligation it is by far the youngest. Along the Eastern Mediterranean the celebration of St. Mary's entrance into heaven seems to have been a common holy day by the sixth century. There it was known as the Falling Asleep, or Dormition, of the Blessed Mother of God, or sometimes as the Transference.

Falling on August 15, the Assumption has increased in importance with the growth of pious legend. Seventh-century tradition tells how Mary's body did not decay when she died but was miraculously transported or *assumed* into heaven. Later accounts pay less attention to her *falling asleep* and more to her *assumption*, describing her as in fact resurrected and serving as Queen of Heaven.

In the Balkans the Assumption is perhaps the greatest saint festival of the year, and to a lesser degree in all the elder daughters of the church — Spain, Portugal, and France, though the Orthodox Church never adopted the tradition of the bodily assumption.

In Sicily there is a kind of bowing procession that marks this day. The Virgin and her Son are carried through the streets in colorful parades. Meeting under an arch of flowers, which symbolizes the gateway to heaven, Jesus bows three times to His Mother. This, say the villagers, indicates His special joy to have her with Him as Queen of Heaven.

In other countries of the Mediterranean, especially in Greece and Portugal, the Assumption is a day to bless the fishing boats and the sponge fleet. All over Europe it was once a day to gather herbs and bless them, that they might more readily heal the sick. When the Assumption was finally regularized as a required feast of the Roman calendar, in the Marian Year of 1950, one of the formal collects for the day recalled the blessing of herbs.

103

THE STATUS OF THE VIRGIN

This roll call of the five major feasts of Mary would not really be complete without a look at Mary's place in the church. As the mother of Christ she certainly deserves great honor. She was God's chosen vessel to bear His Son. The problem therefore is not so much whether we should honor and revere the Virgin Mary but how we can keep the honor and reverence we show her from equaling or displacing that which we owe only to Christ.

The ancient term "Mother of God" or "God-Bearer" *(theotokos)* formulated at the Council of Chalcedon was highly revered not only by the Christians of the Latin and Eastern traditions but with equal fervor by the Reformers. Yet the term can be easily misunderstood. Some theologians, to avoid the connotations that have developed over *theotokos,* prefer the equally ancient and equally reverent term "Mother of Christ" *(Christotokos).*

Whichever term one prefers, what is really significant is what one believes and teaches. If honor for the Virgin tends to crowd out Christ, it is wrong. But if it helps us to understand the human nature of our Lord, our reverence for her can be a worthwhile element of Christian faith.

THE SAINTS IN GENERAL

Today, even in the more liturgical churches, the honor once paid to the great apostles and disciples has lapsed, except perhaps in the great churches of the cities, and even then only when a saint's day happens to fall on a Sunday. Probably this is more the fault of the modern industrial world than of any conscious disregard.

Of saints and of saints' days there are hundreds of varieties. Some, like St. Patrick, belong to a single country — Ireland. Others, like St. Ambrose, were once little known beyond their own diocese — Milan. Some are most famous in the place where they were born — St. Anthony of Padua in Lisbon. Others, like St. George, a native of Asia Minor and patron of England, are more legendary than historic. Still others, like St. Valentine, are really historic but are remembered more for secular reasons than for religious ones. And then there are of course the saints revered generally throughout Christendom.

To assign special days to all the saints, martyrs, apostles, and confessors would take four or five times as many days as there are in the year. Naturally the lesser ones have fallen by the wayside, or are of only local concern.

Yet anyone who calls himself a Christian should know something of the lives and work of those great men and women of God whom in a special way we designate as "saints," even if in most churches, such as the Lutheran, the Anglican, or the Eastern Orthodox, there is no formal process of examination and canonization as in the Roman Catholic Church.

The stories of the saints recall that great "cloud of witnesses" who have led lives that should be an example and an encouragement to all Christians. Even more important, they remind us that we, too, are a part of that "holy catholic church" that is founded on the saints and the apostles, as they learned the faith from the Lord of that church.

St. Andrew the Apostle — November 30

As the brother of Peter, Andrew was one of the earliest and most active of the disciples. Though the Scriptures are silent about his ministry, tradition going back as far as the second century makes him the apostle of Greece and Rumania.

According to tradition he was martyred on a cross in the form of an X, the so-called *saltire* cross. The church at Constantinople counted him as its first bishop and in the year 357 removed his body from its burial place at Patras to Constantinople. His X-shaped cross appears on the spires of Orthodox churches throughout the world and in flags such as the Union Jack.

St. Thomas the Apostle — December 21

Doubting Thomas is one of the more beloved of the disciples, perhaps because we recognize doubt in ourselves. Tradition makes him the patron saint of India and Persia and suggests he may have been buried in Syria. As the patron of the Nestorian church, he was never popular in the West. Doubtless his day is celebrated on December 21st as part of the movement, especially pronounced in the East, to surround the day of our Lord's Nativity with the days of His friends and disciples.

Other saints' days during the Advent season are those of St. Lucy and St. Nicholas, treated in that chapter. St. Stephen, St. John, and the Holy Innocents are in the Christmas Chapter.

St. Valentine — February 14

St. Valentine's Day is of interest not because it was ever a major festival but because the church made use of it to displace a pagan festival it disliked. The Roman season of the Lupercalia celebrated earthly love. Often a youth and a maiden drew lots and then paired off for the year — something like going steady.

105

Seeing the dangers involved, the church substituted the day of one of its minor saints. Eventually the whole tenor of Valentine's Day changed—along with the old name—from sensual and pagan love into hallowed and Christian love. Whether St. Valentine was really interested in young lovers is beside the point. He just happened to die on the right day.

St. Joseph—March 19

St. Joseph's Day, on March 19th, breaks the general rule that saints' days do not intrude into Lent. St. Joseph's Day was seldom celebrated until the 14th or 15th century.

The day seems to have developed in part to support the growing tradition of the perpetual virginity of Mary—that Joseph never joined himself physically to Mary, not even after Jesus' birth. This was once a popular belief among the mystics that has since become doctrine in the Roman and Eastern corpus. In some countries of Europe the considerate bridegroom who lets his wife sleep alone on the bridal night is still spoken of as a "St. Joseph."

Joseph's Day was a big boost for the carpenters guilds since Saint Joseph, the carpenter, was their patron saint. Of all the guilds they alone could host a lively pageant and feast during Lent, when everyone else was restricted from celebrating.

St. Philip and St. James, Apostles—May 1

Of the two disciples Philip and James we know almost nothing. Philip grew up in the same village as Peter and Andrew and made a disciple of Nathaniel. He is not the Philip who preached to the Ethiopian or the deacon of the church at Jerusalem. He is usually pictured with two loaves and a cross, recalling the feeding of the five thousand.

James—"the Less" as he is usually called—is often confused with James, the brother of John, or with James, the brother of our Lord. Often he is pictured with a palm branch or a fuller's staff.

The day of these two apostles recalls the founding of a church in their honor, under John III. In northern Europe May Eve, a night for witches to howl, was sometimes known as *Walpurgisnacht*. Apparently the church elevated the feast of Philip and James to counter the appeal of the pagan festival.

John the Baptist—June 24

John the Baptist's Day fell on June 24th. To the old sun-worshipers of Scandinavia the longest day of the year had always been the biggest holiday of the year, and St. John's Day, under an old form of the calendar, happened to coincide with this day. Like Christmas, his day was celebrated as a major festival, with three services—just after midnight, at dawn, and again later in the morning.

According to Luke, John was six months older than Christ. Saint John's Day therefore had to come six months before Christmas. By the unrevised calendars of the time, Christmas fell on the shortest day of the year, and St. John's Day on the longest—the two most important days of the Teutonic calendar.

Christ heaped high praise on John the Baptist—which He did for none of the Twelve, not even Peter or John. In fact the early church celebrated not just the day John the Baptist was born but also the day he was beheaded, the day he was conceived, and the day he baptized Jesus.

One of the reasons the Scandinavians are such devotees of sunshine and the out-of-doors is that their winter is so dark and snowy. All night long, on St. John's Eve, they tended huge bonfires atop every mountain and lesser ones in every village and courtyard. To the Vikings these fires were a kind of magic.

As they danced about the flames, they thought they were protecting themselves from evil spirits, disease, and plague. These customs closely resemble those of Halloween, when witches are supposed to be out on their brooms and bats are circling belfries.

St. Peter and St. Paul — June 29

The day of St. Peter and St. Paul, celebrated jointly on June 29th, was at one time important. In pious legend Peter and Paul both met death at the hand of Nero in the early sixties, Peter in the Colosseum on a cross and Paul outside the gates, beneath a sword.

According to Duchesne, the June date marks the day Emperor Constantine exhumed their bodies from remote tombs along the Appian Way and returned them to the city. There they were buried in magnificent basilicas the emperor built to their memories, one the prototype of the present St. Peter's and the other St. Paul's Outside the Walls.

The folklore connected with Peter and Paul is so ancient and complex that not even the best of scholars can explain it—their wizardry with snakes, with errant clocks, with poisons, with nonlaying hens, with barking dogs. In northern Europe they often took the place of Woden and Thor, the gods of war and of thunder.

St. Mary Magdalene — July 22

Mary Magdalene is usually thought to be the woman possessed of devils whom Christ once cured. According to John she was the first to greet the Lord on Easter. Tradition sees her living at Ephesus with John and the Virgin Mary. At the time of the Crusades she was one of the most popular of the saints.

St. Lawrence, Martyr — August 10

Lawrence was an important third century pillar of the church in Rome, where he was martyred on a grid. The fact that his date of death was a dividing point in the Pentecost cycle attests his importance — along with St. Peter and St. Paul, and Michael, the Archangel.

He was one of the few non-Biblical saints from the Mediterranean area and won wide popularity in northern Europe, where hundreds of churches bore his name. The meteor showers that occur during the "dog days" of August, also known as the Perseids, were frequently called the "tears of St. Lawrence."

St. Michael and All Angels — September 29

The Feast of St. Michael and All Angels was the occasion for Christians to delight in the colorful legends of the Jews, past masters at revering the angelic host. As the guardian of heaven and God's champion against Satan, St. Michael in some eyes was only one step below the Father. His primary job was to guide the souls of the blessed to heaven, once they had finished their earthly pilgrimage.

This feast really marks the anniversary of a Roman church. The Lutheran reformers added the words "and All Angels" to include four other holy days honoring the angels — the same pattern the Orthodox had followed.

In the Leonine Sacramentary of the sixth century St. Michael's Day had five distinct orders of worship, an honor that was shared only by Christmas and Easter.

Perhaps to get as close to Michael as possible, the faithful built him a shrine on every available mountain, even as the pagan tribes had once built shrines to Woden. This explains how such a remarkable example of the builder's art as that of Mont-Saint-Michel came to be built on the top of a peak in Normandy, out over the tidal flats.

St. Michael won special favor as a guardian of graveyards. In an age when plague, famine, or war often wiped out half a village, Michael was much in the thoughts both of the dying and of those who were left to mourn. With considerable though somewhat ambiguous support from Scriptures, each Christian was thought to have his own guardian angel. Naturally a child would be happier to choose an archangel like Michael rather than some lesser angel whose name he could not even guess.

In Germanic countries the festival fell at the same time as the quarterly meeting of the *Thing* or parliament. The markets, fairs, dancing, feasting, and courts brought in countryfolk for miles around. Michael probably had more mead and beer drunk to his health than all the other inhabitants of heaven put together.

ALL SAINTS AND ALL SOULS — NOVEMBER 1 and 2

Strictly speaking, All Saints' Day is a saints' day, and All Souls is not, though in practice they have always been linked together.

Halloween, or All Saints' Eve was once not a Christian holiday at all, but a Celtic one. Basically the Celts were sun worshipers, and the massive dolmens and circles they built across the face of Europe, like Stonehenge, are still important relics of the pre-Christian era.

It was on their last night of the year, Samhain, October 31st, that the white-robed priests appeased the spirits of the dead. On this night the souls of all who had died during the year roamed abroad, playing tricks on those they had left behind, hexing farm animals, stirring up storms. The easiest way to calm them, according to the Druids, was by potions and fires, by cooking food and leaving it out where they could find it.

This was also the night of witches, of black cats, of owls, and of bats. A pious farmer, if he knew what was good for him, painted a hex sign on the side of his barn, put a consecrated bell round the neck of his cow, and nailed up green willows in the sign of the cross.

The church fought hard to destroy the folk symbols of Halloween — witches, cats, bats, and owls — but with little success. For once, the pagan faith proved the more stable. In fact the Druids were so influential they made mockery of the things they saw on Christian tombstones — especially the skull and the crossbones. In mock rites they even pretended to gather round a human skull and worship it. Many anthropologists think this is the origin of the Halloween pumpkin or Jack-o-lantern — a mocking reverence to the soul of one who has died, represented by the candle.

All Saints is one of the older days in the church calendar. As early as the fourth century St. John Chrysostom boomed out a sermon every year to commemorate all the saints.

Urban IV argued the case for All Saints in this fashion: Since it was obviously a Christian duty to honor the saints, and since even the most pious worshiper might forget one, why not found a single All Saints' Day to cover them all?

When understood in the proper sense, All Saints is one of the most moving days of the year. The sermons and readings often take up the theme that those who died as saints should serve as examples to those left behind.

In the *Book of Common Prayer* Cranmer expressively sums up the mood of All Saints in his Collect: "O Almighty God, who hast knit together Thine elect in one communion and fellowship, in the mystical body of Thy Son, Christ our Lord: Grant us grace so to follow Thy blessed saints in all virtuous and godly living, that we may come to those unspeakable joys, which Thou hast prepared for them that unfeignedly love Thee; through Jesus Christ, our Lord, Amen."

Like Cranmer, the Lutheran reformers retained All Saints' Day, though with reservations. In the year 1527, for example, Luther's extant sermons include those for Nicholas, Anne, Lawrence, Magdalene, Holy Cross, Assumption, Catherine, and John the Baptist, but none for All Saints—probably because he opposed that part of the ritual in which the living prayed for the dead. Prayers directed to God on behalf of the dead, the reformers felt, should be limited to those asking for quiet rest in the grave or comfort for those who had been left behind. They were particularly opposed to the saying of masses for the dead— in fact, any kind of private or votive masses that were not congregational in character.

In contrast to its respect for All Saints, the Reformation sharply condemned All Souls—for a variety of reasons. In medieval Christianity All Souls did for the ordinary Christian what All Saints did for the saint—it annually commemorated all those who had died, especially during the previous year, or in a broader sense, all one's friends and relatives who now lay in the churchyards. In some ways it resembled the American Memorial Day, though without the patriotic overtones. The Latin masses said on this day are known as *requiem* masses, from the word for "rest" (*requiem*) in the introductory words, "Grant unto them eternal rest . . ." The reformers were anxious to restore the New Testament meaning of "saints" as all believers. Thus they would include *all* Christians in celebrating All Saints.

Though it was quite true that the ancient church had prayed both publicly and privately for the souls of the dead, especially in the East, the reformers felt that there was no Scriptural foundation for such prayers and that the custom had been wantonly abused as a source of income.

The monastic orders had pushed the votive masses to a point of scandal, and in many villages All Saints was not so much a day when the grieving family could think good thoughts about their beloved dead as a day when they feared the knock of the monk demanding more money to pray the soul out of purgatory. Despite such excesses, however, the day did serve a useful purpose.

In southern Europe All Souls is often known as Black Vespers. Not only the paraments of the church but also the clothing of the worshipers is black. At home blessed candles send up their flames as a symbol of prayer. In the cemeteries the candles flicker all through the night — a rather touching sight when one sees it for the first time.

St. Martin — November 11

Martin was a French bishop noted for his saintliness in bringing the faith to the valley of the Loire. Born about 316 in the Roman province of Pannonia, now lower Austria, he enlisted in the Roman army. Stationed in Amiens in France, he divided his cloak with a beggar and according to the legend saw a vision of Christ.

His kindliness toward heretics, his reputed miracles, his love for monastic life, and his saintliness soon won him the office of bishop.

This patron of military chaplains was the name-day patron of Martin Luther and one of the most revered of the saints. His feast day was marked with elaborate and generous outlays of food and drink. The Martinmas goose is still a carryover from this ancient feast day.

St. Elizabeth — November 19

Elizabeth was born in Hungary but lived out most of her life (1207 – 1231) in Germany. She is the favorite female saint of almost every German, including Martin Luther and Johann Sebastian Bach.

Her renunciation of the world made her a saint almost in her own lifetime, and within four years of her death she was canonized. In some areas of northern and central Europe she was as famous and revered as the Virgin herself. Her life at the castle of the Wartburg helped hallow also that great landmark of German history — the place where Luther translated the Scriptures and whose courtly history Richard Wagner commemorated in *Tannhäuser*.

*　　　*　　　*

In general, those churches that flowed out of the Reformation have probably been overly conservative in their attitude toward saints' days. From a great surplus of saints and a heavy overlay of legend and superstition, they have swung to the opposite extreme — a total disregard for all those glorious forebears who "did justly and loved mercy and walked humbly with their God." It is still possible to revere them without depending on their good works. It is still possible to remember them without asking that they pray for us. And their lives and witness still serve as an example as we too finish our pilgrimage.

A Final Note

Take an American suburbanite and set him down in the first-century catacombs or in a Roman tenement, and he might never guess he was in a place of worship. On the other hand, take St. Andrew and put him into a modern glass-and-aluminum A-frame with the altar in the middle, and he might never realize this was a church.

Yet both of them, once they heard the words and shared the action of the divine liturgy, would know that they were worshiping. Worship is not a place. Worship is not an altar. Worship is not a crucifix nor a Michelangelo fresco nor a Riemenschneider carving nor a Rouault window.

Worship is basically a remembering, an *anamnesis*. It recalls Christ walking along a path toward Emmaus. It recalls Christ feeding the five thousand. It recalls Christ raising Lazarus. It recalls Christ in the court-yard of Pilate. It recalls Christ on the beams of the cross. It recalls Christ beside the open tomb. It recalls Christ ascending to the right hand of God.

This remembering happens in some degree in private worship, though its full flowering has always been in the public assembly of God's people. In every liturgical act the past merges with the present, and the present with the future, so that all dimensions of time flow together in a blending of the finite and the Infinite, a fusing of the creature with the Creator.

Once Christ had finished his work on earth, He charged the faithful with proclaiming His teachings. To remember Him, to honor Him, and to prepare for His return, the church responded first with a weekly common worship, "not forsaking the assembling of themselves together."

The New Covenant He had made with them focused on the Holy Supper, and here Christ most intimately lived with the faithful. To help

113

them in their remembering, they began to put together verses of Scripture and a primitive liturgy, based on His words and actions.

In time of persecution they used symbols which they thought might help them: the fish, the olive tree, the pelican, flowing water, the ship — all of which we can find engraved on their tombs.

The great mystery of His living and dying and living again, of His coming and going and coming again, they recalled in the Eucharist. Here in the great mystery of God made Man they themselves could share. As He was their *Logos* (word), they were His *logoi* (words). In their suffering they reflected His suffering. In their death they reflected His.

This was of course the emphasis that gave birth to the church year — the Year of the Lord. Each Sunday they recollected His death and His rising. With the passage of time they also thought it wise to celebrate other things He had done — His sending of the Holy Spirit, His baptism, His birth. They also honored those of their own who were now one with Him, prematurely taken from them, the confessors and martyrs.

Today the faithful look back to the church of the apostles with considerable nostalgia. The faith seemed simple then, and on the face of it, easy — as if doubts and disappointments and weaknesses are of modern origin and never afflicted those who had seen the Lord Jesus with their own eyes and heard Him with their own ears.

Sometimes we regret all that has happened to the church in the meantime — the split between East and West, the cleavages within the West, the ornate elaborations of vestment and building and ritual, the secularization and institutionalization and the suburbanization.

In some ways we have followed the pattern of the Hebrews. From a simple trust in a saving and almighty God we have "progressed" to a Pharisaic code that leaves us far worse than when we started. We have intellectualized and philosophized and codified our faith until it is no longer a great mystery calling for a "leap of faith," but a complicated set of propositions.

In the process we appear to be living on the wrong side of Easter, as if Christ died but never rose. Our religious life echoes too much with the *Stabat mater dolorosa,* the grieving Virgin, and not nearly enough with the *Vexilla regis prodeunt,* the victorious banners of our King.

Rather than making of our lives "little Easters," we make them perpetual Good Fridays. Like the Puritans, we ban all sense of joy in our faith, on the grounds that life is sometimes difficult and that therefore God must want us to live as if we are not really enjoying our lot.

But surely this is not our lot. We are God's people. We are His assembly. We are His witnesses. We worship a risen Lord. In our remembering and in our worship we honor those events through which God made us His. For our shortcomings we plead His grace, and for His mighty acts we praise His name. And in that mighty prayer of the church of the apostles we pray: "Even so, come, Lord Jesus." *Maranatha.*